SOCIAL MEDIA
SUCKS!

(IF YOU DON'T KNOW WHAT YOU'RE DOING)

SOCIAL MEDIA
SUCKS!

(IF YOU DON'T KNOW WHAT YOU'RE DOING)

SEBASTIAN RUSK

FOREWORD BY *NEW YORK TIMES*
BEST-SELLING AUTHOR
JAY BAER

Published by Advantage, Charleston, South Carolina.
Member of Advantage Media Group.

ADVANTAGE is a registered trademark and the Advantage colophon is a trademark of Advantage Media Group, Inc.

Printed in the United States of America.

ISBN: 978-159932-471-5
LCCN: 2014935716

This publication is designed to provide accurate and authoritative information in regard to the subject matter covered. It is sold with the understanding that the publisher is not engaged in rendering legal, accounting, or other professional services. If legal advice or other expert assistance is required, the services of a competent professional person should be sought.

Advantage Media Group is proud to be a part of the Tree Neutral® program. Tree Neutral offsets the number of trees consumed in the production and printing of this book by taking proactive steps such as planting trees in direct proportion to the number of trees used to print books. To learn more about Tree Neutral, please visit www.treeneutral.com. To learn more about Advantage's commitment to being a responsible steward of the environment, please visit www.advantagefamily.com/green

Advantage Media Group is a publisher of business, self-improvement, and professional development books and online learning. We help entrepreneurs, business leaders, and professionals share their Stories, Passion, and Knowledge to help others Learn & Grow. Do you have a manuscript or book idea that you would like us to consider for publishing? Please visit advantagefamily.com or call 1.866.775.1696.

FOREWORD

The speed equation is the component of social media that most people get hopelessly wrong. Because the mechanics of social media happen instantaneously, the natural expectation is that results accrue the same way: at the snap of the fingers, or at the blink of an eye.

But in reality, social media results are, typically, compiled over time, not created overnight. It's the difference between filling a bucket one drop at a time with a dripping faucet or instantly filling it with a fire hose. A fire hose is faster, but what are the chances you have a fire hose lying around? Everyone has a faucet, and in this extraordinary book, my friend Sebastian Rusk shows you exactly how he filled his social media success bucket to *overflowing*, one drop at a time over a period of years.

Does that sound disappointing? Does it frighten you that it took years of hard work for the author to become a leading social media practitioner? Then, maybe this isn't the book for you. If you want a "recipe for becoming a huge social media success in 90 days or less," you can certainly find one. They are all over the Internet, just waiting for people to plunk down $50 or $100 or $1,500 via their PayPal accounts, only to find out later that the fire hose is a pipe dream. Instead, if you want to know how social media success actually happens in the real world, this book is a terrific investment (and an entertaining one, as well).

One of the other big misunderstandings about social media is that you can conquer it in your underpants. While the ability to participate in social media anytime and anywhere via a mobile device makes it a very flexible platform of opportunity, the truth is that social media works best when it's *part* of your story and a *portion* of your business plan, not all of it. Social media is an ingredient in your success, not the entire entrée.

What you'll realize when reading *Social Media Sucks!* is how intuitively and effectively Sebastian utilizes offline, face-to-face exchanges to build and expand his platform. Whether it's his extremely recognizable personal branding "hook" to get you to remember him, his use of video interviews to get him into your inner circle, or his ability to walk into a nail salon and sell the owner a framed Monet poster, Sebastian demonstrates the power of the in-person approach, and shows you how to do it for yourself.

You'll also find in this book a collection of relevant examples of companies and brands that are adept and nimble and dynamic and interesting in social media (in addition to the author's personal use of the medium, of course). I particularly enjoy how Sebastian presents these successes in a straightforward, easy-to-understand fashion. You'll be inspired by these tales, and you'll be able to borrow ideas and inspiration that you can use in your own social media, or in social media on behalf of your business.

Lastly, I should acknowledge that there are far too many books that overcomplicate social media. As Sebastian's personal success journey demonstrates, many of the same principles that were chronicled in Dale Carnegie's day still apply now; they are just magnified by social media. Be useful. Be kind. Be aware. Be persistent. Be timely. Be imaginative. Be empathetic. Know your customers and their motivations and needs. It all makes sense, then and now.

What most authors don't want you to know is that social media isn't hard; it's just complicated. There are many moving parts and details, and ways to do things incrementally better (or worse) in social media. But at its core, social media success is about people and passion, and as you'll see in the pages that follow, nobody is more qualified on those two points than Sebastian Rusk.

I know you'll enjoy *Social Media Sucks!*, and I'm eager for you to dive in!

Very best regards, and I'll see you on Twitter (and beyond).

Jay Baer

New York Times best-selling author of *Youtility: Why Smart Marketing Is About Help, Not Hype*

@jaybaer

TABLE OF CONTENTS

INTRODUCTION

This book is intended to help people know what they "don't know that they don't know" about social media. It's for people who don't know where to begin or even what questions to ask. This book is for people who know nothing about social media beyond the fact that they have a Facebook page, and that a thing called Twitter exists. But it is not just for them. It is also for active social media users who want to improve their game.

My goal, the thing I do every day of my life, is to help people better understand the amazing power of social media. I want people to understand that social media is something we have always engaged in. The only difference is, today we have tools such as Facebook, Twitter, blogs, and YouTube, among many others. But the reality is we have only truly had those things at our disposal since about 2005, give or take a year or two.

Social media is our face to the world, our image, whether that image reflects a business or our personal brands—the business of us, or, the business of you. Social media is important because of this simple truth: we do business with people we know, like, and trust. Social media allows us to validate desirable qualities in the people we do business with and, more importantly, the people we decide to interact with and associate ourselves with in everyday life.

Social media can help you do three key things:

1. build an online community,
2. engage with that community, and
3. become the go-to source within your community or your industry.

When you build a community, you meet new people who have similar interests, you engage with people who have similar interests, and you become the go-to source for people who have similar interests. You become an authority in whatever it is you do.

You build a community by finding like-minded individuals. When they share things, you enjoy them. When you share things, they enjoy them. Eventually, the circle widens and others join the community. You engage with them when you "like," comment on, and share the content they have sent out, and eventually they do the same for you.

Not only is social media designed for you to become that go-to source, but it can also help you find your go-to sources. We have all got our go-to sources and we use them to help us get to where we want to be.

MY BACKSTORY

I did not go to college. I knew that there was a better way for me. Everyone was excited to go off to college for another four years of school. I said to myself, "They couldn't keep me in school when it was free. Why in the world would I ever want to go if I have to pay for it?"

I soon found out that I was a natural-born salesman. I learned this early on. When I was growing up in Miami, the owner of the condo where my mom and I were living sold the unit out from under us. We had about two months to find a new place to live. I decided to pick up the newspaper and thumb through the local rental listings. It was just my mom and me. She worked 40-plus hours a week and had enough to do on top of that as a single mom. I asked myself, "How hard could it be to pick up a newspaper, call some real estate agents and locate a new place for us to live?"

I did just that. I found us a three-bedroom, two-bathroom townhouse less than a mile from where we had been living. The listing agent sat me down. I think I was 15 or 16 years of age at the time. He said, "Hey, kid, you should really think about getting your real estate license." Boy, I should have listened to him. I never ended up getting my real estate license, but that exchange did open my eyes to a few big ideas.

I thought, "This guy is successful. He seems to know what he's talking about in business. Maybe he is on to something. Maybe he sees something in me that I haven't yet realized myself." I eventually started to understand that I had been ingrained with a gift, the gift of being a natural salesman. Years later, that led to my realization that I had a larger gift—the gift of being a businessman.

In addition to the impression that that real estate agent made on me, there was the close family friend of ours who owned the Corvettes. He was an attorney, a very successful one, and every couple of years he would buy a brand new Corvette to replace the previous one. The day we threw my sister a college graduation party, he had a turquoise Corvette. I remember it as if it were yesterday. This was maybe 1995 or 1996, and I think I was 15 years old. I jokingly said to him, "Hey, Danny, let me take it for a spin." He reached into his pocket, pulled out the keys, and threw them to me. I thought, "What in the world? Is this guy crazy?" And then I said it out loud. "Are you crazy?" He said, "No, kid. I want to give you a good taste of what you can get and what you can have if you work hard."

The thing about that car was the faster you went, the louder the radio got. I took that thing for a spin, a serious spin, and, thankfully, did not wreck it. Moments like those helped reassure me, helped solidify my belief in my gift. They helped me understand that I had something special. I found out later that what I had was the gift of entrepreneurship, because, in my opinion, the true definition of an entrepreneur is "a natural-born salesman and businessman rolled into one."

I did not realize the entrepreneur side of things until I was about 24 or 25 years old, but I did understand the sales aspect and the hustle aspect. I never got that out of my head. I told myself, "I'm either going to be a successful real estate agent one day when I get my real estate license, or I'm going to be a successful salesman." Those were the two roads I saw ahead of me. I chose to travel the road of sales.

My first real sales job was selling artwork door to door. I'll never forget it. I moved to Tampa, Florida, and saw an ad in the paper that read, "Rock and roll atmosphere, free beer, apply here." I thought that looked pretty cool. I called the number and set up an interview.

I walked in. The Beastie Boys were cranking. This big, tall, Italian guy with huge hands walked out to greet me. His name was Joe, but his nickname was Mitts, because his hands were so big that they looked like baseball mitts. They had offices all around the country and operated sort of like the guys who sell stereo speakers out of the trunks of their cars. The only difference was these guys did it with artwork.

I was hungry. I was 18 years old. I wasn't making any money and I was sick of working at McDonald's and other odd jobs. This place seemed really cool. My only problem was that I did not have a car. I said, "Hey listen, I'd love to go do this, but I don't have a car." Mitts said, "No problem. I'm going to send you out with somebody tomorrow. You can see what it's all about. The following day I'll send you out with somebody else. You can work alongside him and we'll work it out from there."

I did that for a couple of days. By the third day, I was so amped up, Mitts would have to peel me off of the ceiling every single day. I finally came in and said, "Listen, I can do this but we need to figure something out. I found a car on the side of the road that's for sale for $500."

That Saturday, Mitts went with me and actually bought me that car. I loaded it up with artwork and I was off to the races. I would knock on doors everywhere around Tampa, Clearwater, Ocala—you name it. Some days, I would even drive to Orlando. I would run into a business and say, "I'm sorry for bothering you. My boss just sent me over. We're clearing out our warehouse. I have a bunch of artwork framed in glass, *this big* … for $20." At this point, I would spread my arms out to show them how big the pictures were. They would all perk up, and I would say, "Let's go, ladies. Grab your cigarettes and checkbooks. Let's go check them out. I've got Dalís, Monets, Van Goghs. I've got a couple velvet, weeping Elvises. I've got exactly what you need."

Even if they told me they didn't have enough space on their wall for any more artwork, I told them that the pictures were small enough to fit in between the washer and dryer and underneath the bed. Needless to say, that job really gave me the true grit I needed to be able to understand what hustling was all about. Was selling artwork door to door really an admirable or enviable way to earn a living? Was it something that a person would want to rant and rave about? Probably not. But knocking on doors every day and having them slammed in my face for $5 a picture kept me constantly motivated and focused.

Back then, the whole mentality of being burned down and brought up every day in the sales room was okay. These days, people tend to frown on that. But I really built the foundation of my hustle by getting knocked down and pulling myself back up again. Fast-forward a couple of years. I ended up starting life a little earlier than the norm when I had a child at age 22. I guess the science experiment worked. When I learned I was going to be a father, I started to work for an Internet company and entered the dot-com space. I got another opportunity in Chicago. I moved to Chicago and entered the real dot-com space.

My daughter was born. I lived in Chicago for a year, and one night I was up at three o'clock in the morning with her. I had been working for a domain registrar in Chicago called ItsYourDomain. com, and in those wee hours of that one morning, as I sat there with my daughter, I saw an infomercial that offered to help people go into business for themselves online. I thought, "Whoever is behind this product is obviously registering domain names," and that is exactly what I was doing at the time. I was going after large accounts that were registering large amounts of domain names. It was my job to get out there and develop business.

I called the guy who was behind the infomercial and he never answered. I kept calling him, for six months, and finally one day he picked up the phone. He gave me the Michael Douglas line from the movie *Wall Street*. "Kid, your picture should be under the word 'persistent' in the dictionary. I absolutely want to do business with you, but before we discuss doing business, have you ever thought about moving to Southern California?" I said, "Wait a minute, buddy. I just had a baby. I'm 22 years old. I just moved to the frozen tundra of Chicago a year ago and I don't know if I'm going to go anywhere."

He said, "Alright, well, you let me know." I tried to get the deal done for six months. It never came to fruition. Six months later, I had been in Chicago for a year and I was freezing. I said, "I've got to get back to the beach. I'm either going East or I'm going West." I called the infomercial guy in Southern California again and he picked up the phone and said, "You're ready, aren't you?" I said, "I'm considering it." He said, "Listen, why don't you get here and we'll sit down and we'll talk about it."

I said, "Wait a second. You're looking for a salesman. I'm not looking for a job. I'm just calling to ask you more about what you're looking for." He said, "Well, you get out here." I ended up going out there. I was supposed to go for the weekend, but I ended up staying three weeks. I went in and absolutely crushed it with my sales ability. I understood the concept of people going into business on the Internet. I understood people registering domain names. Most importantly, I understood the power of the phone ringing all day after people had seen something on television and wanted to buy it and capitalize on it.

Needless to say, I quickly became the top salesman. I worked there for a year and the guy who owned the company and had hired me told me that at 24 years old I would make my first hundred grand. That actually happened. I made $103,000 and change that year. I knew I could do it. I won the salesman-of-the-year title. I went to the Caribbean on a cruise, came back, and quit.

People thought I was absolutely out of my mind. They said, "What are you doing? You're the top salesman. You run the show here. You usually make six figures. You're a young guy." I said, "Yeah, but if I can make a hundred grand for this guy, how much could I make for myself?"

So I quit, and as the real estate market started to thrive, I knew there was some opportunity there. I got into the direct-marketing space for mortgage brokers and realtors. I started developing direct-marketing campaigns that would bring borrowers and potential buyers directly to the brokers' doorsteps. I did that for about three and a half years until the market crashed in 2008. I did exceptionally well, tripled my income, and was truly my own boss. I had arrived at entrepreneurship.

But I soon found out that I had built a brand within that direct-marketing space that was not sustainable. I had built a brand that did not have a light at the end of the tunnel. I was making a lot of money, creating a lifestyle, and then the bottom fell out because the market crashed. There was nobody to sell my product to anymore, yet all of my bill collectors wanted their bills paid at the end of the month.

I found myself back in South Florida for a friend's wedding in early 2008. I woke up on Miami Beach—not literally on the beach, but in a friend's house—and said to myself, "You know what? It's time to come home." That weekend I ended up hanging out with another friend who was doing exceptionally well with his business. We discussed my moving back to Miami and he said he wanted to help me facilitate that move because he knew the ground was falling out from underneath me.

I was supposed to return to California in March 2008 and then come back to Miami in July, after I had worked out the details and logistics of the move. It was a big move—West Coast to East Coast—and I figured it would take at least a few months to sort out and plan. I found out when I returned to California that I was completely emotionally checked out and there was no need to do much more thinking or planning. I decided to sell everything I owned on Craigslist. I was back in Miami a month later.

It took me two years to wrap my head around the fact that I had gotten a taste of success and had lost it all because of poor planning. I sat around and sulked for two years until I realized I had to do something about it. I told myself, "If I did it once, if I got to the top of the mountain once, I can get back to the top of the mountain again." But then I asked myself, "How am I going to do that?" As any good entrepreneur who is pulling himself out of the mud does, I took a huge liking to personal development.

I had always been a fan of Anthony Robbins. I called a friend of mine who worked for Tony Robbins in California, and I asked about Tony's upcoming event in Long Beach, California. This was in the summer of 2008. I got all the details. Then she said, "Hey, by the way, I have a good friend who lives in Miami and travels with Tony. She'd be a great contact for you." My friend quickly put the two of us in touch, and I decided that week to film a video about what I was doing at the time.

I was still working on direct marketing efforts (some of them left over from my time in California), but I was working twice as hard for half of the money. So I recorded a video of myself talking about my direct marketing efforts, and planned to send it out to my prospects list of 90 or 100 people. It was sort of a video calling card.

Before I sent it out, I decided to show it to my new friend and she absolutely blew up. She said, "You need to start a YouTube show. I think you would be great at it, and it would be a huge success." I thought, "Well, what am I going to talk about? Direct marketing efforts within the real estate mortgage area?"

As we know, in 2008 and 2009, "mortgage" and "real estate" were not happy words. I had been messing around on MySpace since early 2005, but I thought, "Hold on a second. I do know a lot about social media. There is a lot of buzz around social media. Social media, there's a lot of social buzz ... SocialBuzzTV.com!"

Three days later, I said those three words to my designer, and soon I had what is now the logo of SocialBuzzTV.com. I had an idea and a company name, but how in the world was I going to make money? I had no idea, but I told myself that if I made enough noise, someone would come knocking on my door.

WHERE I WENT FROM THERE
WITH MY BRAND

Now, mind you, I had lost basically everything. I moved back to Miami in 2008 with a duffel bag and my daughter. I did not have a car. I had a bus pass and a skateboard, but that was really all I had for transportation. I bought a flip-camera on Amazon for $80, and I told myself I would start videoing every event I went to. I would also start hyping up my SocialBuzzTV.com show on YouTube, telling everybody, "It's going to be the best show ever." I was sure if I made that noise, someone would knock on my door. I started going to networking events in Miami and spreading the word, telling anyone I could about what I was up to.

They would ask, "What's your revenue stream? How do you make money?" I would say, "I have no idea." My plan was just to go to networking events, take out my flip-camera, put together a one- or two-minute video recap of the event and brand it with my logo. I would then say to the event organizers, "Hey, listen, I'm going to give you this video for free in exchange for you telling everybody about me."

I rode the bus all over town with my flip-camera, and I attended every event I could. Then I started to think, "Hold on a second. If this guy's doing an event, how come I can't do an event? How hard could it be?"

Soon, I was going to local restaurants and saying, "Hey, listen, can you let me do a networking event here in that little area over there? I'm going to bring between 30 and 40 people here on a night that you're not that busy, on Monday or Tuesday night, if you could just help with appetizers and maybe a free cocktail for my guests. I'm sure it'll be mutually beneficial, because the event will last for a couple of hours and people will spend money at your venue." They quickly agreed to that.

Those nighttime networking events soon evolved into daytime seminars and social media boot camps, often in the same restaurants with many of the same people who had shown up on previous nights. I also invited people I had met at other events. I would say to the venue managers, "Let me have that room in the back of the restaurant next Monday morning from nine to twelve," and again they quickly agreed.

One event fed off the other. I was promoting my own events at my events. There is a concept for you! The people who attended my social media boot camps did not pay a lot of money. I would charge, I think, anywhere from $30 to $50 per camp. Sometimes, I was presenting my seminar to five people. Other times it was 15 people. But any amount of income was significant, because it was my first opportunity to generate revenue for SocialBuzzTV.com. People were paying me to tell them what I knew about Facebook and Twitter and YouTube and blogs.

Eventually, people started saying, "Hey, you obviously know what you're talking about with this social media stuff. Maybe you can help me set up my own social media." So in November 2011, we launched the SocialBuzzTV.com agency, which enabled us to help people set up their Facebook page, their Twitter account, their blog account. We were able to help them set up a YouTube page, shoot some videos, and start developing their social media campaigns.

Back in 2011, social media was still the Wild Wild West. It was a mysterious frontier, and people didn't get it, so they were slow to dive in. I was quick to dive in and then I committed myself to helping others join me on the other side of that largely uncharted frontier.

So that's my path in a nutshell. That is how I was able to go from "salesman" to "businessman" to "entrepreneur" to someone who thought he was the next Donald Trump and then lost it all. I went from top gun to squirt gun and on my way back to top gun, I built a brand from absolutely nothing. The next time you think, "I've lost it all and I don't think I'll ever get it back," remember that there is always an opportunity to point you back to the top of the mountain, especially when you have already been there.

I also want to backtrack a little bit here and tell you about one more factor in my rise back to the top of the mountain. A huge contributing factor of my building SocialBuzzTV.com was not only my friend who motivated me to start my own YouTube channel, but also a book that came into my life in 2010. A friend called me and said, "You've got to check out this book. It's titled *Crush It! Why Now Is the Time to Cash in on Your Passion* and it's by this guy Gary Vaynerchuk. The guy's energy is exactly the same as yours. You'll totally hit it off with him."

So my friend gave me the audio version of the book and I started listening to it every day. With that book, released in the fall of 2009, Gary created a blueprint for launching a brand from nothing just by utilizing the free tools and resources that social media has to offer.

The subtitle of the book basically explains it all: *Why Now Is the Time to Cash in on Your Passion.* Now is the time to do it. The book basically says, whatever your interest is, start writing about it and blogging about it. That really allowed the antennae on my head to go up. I decided that I wanted to crush it too, so I continued to follow Gary.

A year and a half went by. He came out with a second book, *The Thank-You Economy.* I contacted his office to request an interview with him at the Miami stop of his book tour. I also got in touch with a professional camera crew, and they agreed to collaborate with me. I thought I was going to talk to Gary for a couple of minutes in the hallway. He came in and was more than cordial and said, "Whatever we need to do to shoot this piece, we can do." I spent about an hour with him before his book signing.

I had the opportunity to thank Gary for writing *Crush It* and for the impact he had on me and my brand. He was the one who caused my antennae to go up and to become aware of some pretty important ideas. I completely admire Gary and his work. If you do not know who Gary Vaynerchuk is, you need to. Check him out online at www.garyvaynerchuk.com. If you're reading this, Gary, thanks again for everything.

The Birth of
the Brand—and
the Bow Tie

F or me, it all started with a video. I was doing a lot of direct marketing for real estate companies when I really began to become an entrepreneur and when I conceptualized what is known today as SocialBuzzTV.com. I decided that a good way to attract new clients would be through the use of video.

It was getting easier and easier to shoot videos, to capture memories, and literally document a brand via online video. With YouTube being the number-two search engine on the planet, a product of Google and constantly growing, I knew that online video was not slowing down at all.

Being able to connect and interact with Gary Vaynerchuk, who built and grew his brand through video, was a huge opportunity. I really trusted the path he was on and knew that I could do something similar. I shot a video at home and sent it out to prospective clients in the real estate, mortgage, and debt consolidation industry, claiming that I could increase their business. I got lots of positive responses based on that, but I knew I could do more with the video. I wanted to build a brand.

When I bought that flip-cam and started running around in Miami to every networking event in town, video was something that I could use to brand the daylights out of what I was doing, promoting other peoples' events on SocialBuzzTV.com. So that is what I did. I began to turn my flip-cam habit into a consumable "thing." In other words, I began to turn it into a brand.

But after going to everybody else's events, I wanted to start doing my own, so that was my next step. I approached a local restaurant with a bar and told the manager I could bring 30 or 40 people there on a Monday or Tuesday night when the place was dead. The restaurant manager liked the idea, because my guests would be buying cocktails and food. So, all of a sudden, I had a free event venue. The restaurant would get exposure and I would, too, when I told all of my guests about the restaurant via SocialBuzzTV.com.

Of course, I shot videos of my event because I wanted to document that process and promote future events. I was sure that after I had captured the feeling of the event, which video does such a good job of, people who had not attended the event would say, "I need to make it to the next event." And that is what happened. My brand grew, and my audience grew.

Sometimes I even had local news stations contact me, wanting to use my video content on the evening news. As we all know, local media is completely unpredictable, so none of my videos ever aired, but the mere fact that the media asked for them further solidified my belief that the power of video was real.

When a colleague of mine saw the first video I had shot at home for my prospective direct-marketing clients, she insisted I start my own YouTube channel. She said I had great energy and was able to clearly convey my message. I appreciated her enthusiasm and I was encouraged, but I wondered what in the world I would talk about on my own YouTube channel. I certainly would not be talking about real estate marketing in 2008 and 2009, the industry's all-time low in my lifetime. After all, I wanted to stay in business.

Then it hit me. I had been an early adopter of social media. I could share my thoughts about social media. It was kind of like talking about talking, or writing about writing, but lots of people do that and enjoy great success. Why couldn't I do the same with social media? I knew that I had the ability to teach people what they "didn't know that they didn't know," and I believe when you do that, people do business with you. When people do business with you, you make money. When you make money, you are successful.

The name SocialBuzzTV.com popped into my head, and three days later a designer was presenting me with what is now the logo for SocialBuzzTV.com. Buying that Kodak pocket-video flip-camera for $80 on Amazon allowed me to show up at events and document them, organize and document my own events, and really start to build the brand that would become SocialBuzzTV.com.

In addition to being able to leverage video to tell the story of your brand, the sharing capability of online video is ridiculous. If someone has seen your video and enjoyed it, we all know what happens next. They share it. They post it, retweet it, and blog about it. It might even end up being utilized by the local news outlet. The opportunities are absolutely endless with online video. Most videos today do not even require a flip-cam. You can shoot most video with your smartphone. You can even upload it directly to YouTube, Facebook, and a number of other platforms, with just a couple of clicks on a smartphone—and you can do it within minutes of shooting the video.

So, after attending and videoing several networking events, I started hosting my own events. But even then, I wanted to take it a step further. I wanted to present a social media boot camp, and I wanted to do it at that same venue where I hosted my networking events. I wanted to stay fresh in peoples' minds. I wanted to stay top of mind. I believe there is a lot of power in staying top of mind, but most importantly, I want to share my knowledge and help people "know what they don't know that they don't know."

My events were doing well, attracting more people each time, and I began inviting those people back a week later to attend my social media boot camp. I would charge $30 to $50 and I would teach them everything I knew about Facebook, Twitter, YouTube, and blogs. The boot camps were extremely well received.

Soon, people were offering me $300 to $500 to set up and manage their Facebook and Twitter accounts on a monthly basis. They would say, "I've been to your events," or "I met you at another event," or "I've been to your boot camp. You obviously know what you're talking about." That part of my business was unexpected, but it gave birth to yet another aspect of my brand—SocialBuzzTV.com agency. The agency now handles the setup, management strategy, and community growth of all social media needs for a variety of businesses and brands.

For more information on how our agency works, check out our deck here: http://bit.ly/SBAgency

We have had the opportunity to work with brands that we resonate with, brands that we like and get excited about. Never in my wildest dreams did I think a little YouTube show aimed at educating people about social media would turn into a scalable brand, but it did. That in itself proves the power of social media. What I learned through all of it, and what this book is going to teach you to do, can be summed up this way: trust the process, do the work, and the money will come.

THE BIRTH OF THE BOW TIE

In addition to going to events, hosting my own events and presenting boot camps and seminars, the way I wanted to stay top of mind and stand out was by wearing big black Poindexter glasses. I started wearing them around town constantly and people thought I was completely nuts. But I wore them. Whether I was nuts or not, people remembered me. "Oh, that was the guy with the big thick glasses on," they would say. I have 20/20 vision, so there is no real need for me to wear glasses, and after every hipster in Miami started wearing similar glasses, I had to retire them.

So I needed something new. Having worked on an online project that educates people about social media, called the SocialBuzzUniversity.com, I thought maybe I would call myself the social media professor. When I thought of the word *professor*, I automatically associated it with a bow tie for some reason.

I was shooting a couple of videos for the online social media education piece, and I decided to put a bow tie on. I had no idea how to tie it, but I learned how. And just how did I learn to tie a bow tie, you might ask? Well, I learned how to tie a bow tie from YouTube. Could anything be more perfect than that? It took me about an hour, but I kept watching the video over and over until I got it right. It was yet another great example of the power of online video and, of course, YouTube specifically.

With a correctly tied bow tie under my chin, I looked at myself in the mirror and said, "You know what? I can go out in public like this. I can hold my head up high and attend an event, host an event or present a seminar wearing this bow tie and people will take me seriously." I was convinced that the bow tie had replaced the glasses.

> PRO TIP: Again, if you do not remain top of mind, people will forget about you. I think Steve Martin was once quoted as saying, "Be so good they can't forget you." They can forget about you overnight. They can forget about you within a matter of hours. I did not want that to happen. I was in the midst of building a brand from absolutely nothing and the bow tie was going to help me stay top of mind. The bow tie was going to help me continue to stand out and build my brand.

These days, I cannot really leave the house without a bow tie. In the rare cases that I do, people say, "Where's the bow tie, Sebastian?" The large and prestigious brand Perry Ellis was sending me bow ties from its new collection. If I wore a Perry Ellis bow tie while shooting a video, the company managers knew that I would be talking about them. Perry Ellis is a large brand. Its management understands the value of people talking about them. But I think it is important to understand exactly how I established that relationship with Perry Ellis in the first place.

I was heading down to Miami Beach one morning for a run. (I always bring my phone with me when I go for a run, because I like to take pictures.) As I approached the beach, I took a picture of a little walkway entrance. It was the perfect beach landscape: a wooden walkway onto the sand. Behind it was a lifeguard station and then the ocean. I posted the picture on Instagram and also tweeted it and posted it on Facebook. James Brown from Perry Ellis (headquartered in Miami) quickly commented, "Wow, that picture looks like another Perry Ellis ad."

Then James said something that started with "Unfortunately …" and ended with "that's all about to change with our new spring collection coming out." As a joke I wrote, "I hope there are bow ties involved," to which came the reply, "How did you know?"

A week later, James Brown, the head of marketing for Perry Ellis in Miami, direct-messaged me on Twitter and asked for my contact information. He wanted to send a few bow ties to me. I did not think much of it. That was until the FedEx man knocked on my door. I had a package from Perry Ellis with five brand-new bow ties from the spring collection, a key chain and a handwritten note from my new buddy, James, at Perry Ellis: "Thanks in advance for wearing these bow ties. We really hope you enjoy them."

I knew I had something here. Not only had I put a bow tie on and gone out in public, but people had taken me seriously when I did it. I knew this was going to be a symbol of my brand, that people would start associating SocialBuzzTV.com and me with bow ties. It was something that was really going to resonate with people. It was real.

It was clear that what I was doing was starting to resonate with large brands. They understood the power of real-time social buzz. They understood the power of a guy like me wearing a bow tie around town, talking about their brand and endorsing their brand by default, simply by talking about exactly what I was doing: wearing their bow tie.

Was I trying to sell Perry Ellis bow ties through this whole process? Absolutely not. All I was trying to do was help people better understand, once again, the power of social media and the power of someone telling the story of a brand. I had not known that I was going to come across an opportunity like this when I woke up that morning and went down to the beach for a run. I snapped that picture and posted it on Instagram just because I thought it was beautiful. But everything that followed is evidence of the power of social media.

You never know who is watching, you never know who might respond or interact. Even more importantly, you never know what type of creative ideas you are going to be able to come up with based on your day-to-day interactions, both offline and online. I am really grateful I was able to put down the glasses and put on a bow tie. In addition to the Perry Ellis relationship, there have been numerous other relationships I have been able to develop thanks to my signature bow tie. As my good friend and branding virtuoso Bruce Turkel says, the bow tie is not my brand, but it is certainly an extension of my brand and something people associate me with.

I attended the SocialFresh.com conference in Tampa, Florida, for the first time about a year and a half ago. One of the speakers at the conference was Scott Monty, Global Digital & Multimedia Communications for Ford Motor Company, and now a good friend of mine. Scott wears bow ties as if it's his job to do that, and he rocks them well. At the conference, I was able to connect with him and interview him, and, of course, our mutual affinity for bow ties gave us an almost instant rapport.

One of the first things he said to me was, "Sebastian, remember, bow ties never go out of style because bow ties were never in style." Not only did I find that hilarious, it also connected us instantly. My interview touched on several topics, from the dream job Scott was enjoying at Ford to his ability to proudly rock the bow tie, and all of it helped me stay connected to him moving forward.

Six months later, I was at an event in Miami. I was wearing a bow tie and I ran into some people from the agency for Ford in the Southeast. One of the representatives from the agency approached me and said, "Hey, I think you interviewed our Global Digital & Multimedia Communications for Ford Motor Company, Scott Monty, earlier this year at the SocialFresh.com conference."

I said, "I most definitely did. I love what Scott's doing. I love his complement to the Ford brand, and I definitely love his bow ties." He said, "We love his bow ties as well, and we also love yours and we want to do business with you."

A few months later, as part of a marketing campaign promoting the 2013 Ford Escape, Ford decided to sponsor a Miami area SocialBuzzTV.com event that I was hosting. I not only got paid for allowing Ford to sponsor my event, but was also able to leverage the Ford name with SocialBuzzTV.com. I got to align my brand with one of the most established and successful brands in the world. Once again, I was reassured about the bow tie. My decision to take a chance and start wearing a bow tie to events was validated. The look was memorable, sustainable and it was now bringing in revenue. I don't think I'll ever stop wearing bow ties—ever.

Social Media
Happens Offline
and Online

B eing social is nothing new. Humans have socialized since the beginning of time. Think about the caveman's campfire, the crier in the town square, the corner barbershop, and the Internet—all venues for communication. Our desire to be social and share ideas has never lost its appeal. In fact, it has only increased with time.

Being social is something we humans have always done. We engage in "social media" every day, even if we do not touch an electronic device. We meet for coffee or lunch with clients. We sit through strategic meetings and bounce ideas off each other. We agree on and execute business transactions.

We also do things as simple as walking out of our houses and saying hello to our neighbors, garbage men, or postal workers. Some of us start our days in coffee shops, where we greet baristas by saying "Good morning." All of these things are social. Nothing has changed in the way we are social, except for the way the messages are delivered.

We did not have these tools or resources ten years ago, around 2004. They are all relatively brand new. Social media is now scalable and at our fingertips, but it has always been around in some form or another. Facebook, Twitter, and blogs are simply the new tools and message delivery systems for a concept that is as old as humankind.

Even in modern times, pre-Internet, there was a social media network in place. In the 1950s, if Bob's Butcher Shop sold a bad batch of meat, every customer in town knew about it and would not shop at Bob's again until they knew Bob had corrected the issue. Remember, social media did not even exist until around 2005. Technically, the year was late 2004, with the launch of LinkedIn.com, but it took a while for people to catch on—and some still haven't caught on, unfortunately. It was not until about 2007 that people really understood what they could do with it.

In 1999, Bill Gates said (and I am paraphrasing), "Any business that doesn't have a website in 2000 will not be in business." But even then, social media was unheard of. The Internet picked up steam and started to become mainstream, but still some people were skeptical. Chat rooms followed, and next came cell phones, texting, and Internet access on smartphones. We all know what that did to us. Now, the average American cannot be more than three feet away from his phone at any give time. It's sad, but true.

I think it is very important to point out the relevancy of Bill Gates's prediction in 1999: *If you are in business and you don't have a website in the year 2000, you aren't in business.* I think you could say the same thing in 2014 about online social media. If you are a business in 2014 and you don't have a social media presence, you aren't in business.

If prospective customers are looking to do business with you and they land on your outdated website and have no ability to connect with you instantaneously in other places such as Facebook, Twitter, YouTube, Google+, or blogs, they will probably move on and continue their search. If they have the ability to connect with the next business in line—namely, your competition—they might just take their business there. Imagine if a prospective customer is able to find out more about you and your business by reading your blog, or watching your videos and connecting with you on Facebook, or following you on Twitter. Any of those things is going to help a customer make an educated, conscious decision about whether or not to do business with you. If you have relevant content available to your prospective customer online, it will help your cause. If you have nothing or subpar products and information available to your customer, it will make his decision easy. He will simply move on and explore a relationship with your competition.

Where does that leave you? That leaves you left out in the cold. Why? Because you decided that social media is not important to your brand. *Do not* miss the boat on this and *do not* miss the importance of understanding these very fundamental concepts. Social media is where we are right now and where we will continue to be. It is not going anywhere. The Genie is not going back into the bottle. Considering the billion-dollar valuations of Facebook and Twitter, in my opinion, this is not just another tech bubble happening. This is reality. This is the way it is, and it is only going to grow and become more relevant.

As Mark Zuckerberg said when he first launched Facebook, people want an area in which they can communicate and share the happenings of their life. Facebook, Twitter, YouTube, blogs, and the multiple other social platforms allow us to do just that. At every juncture, each time one of the above technologies was introduced, a sector of society was skeptical and late to adopt. But soon, each of these things became part of everyday life. We could even go back further and apply the same pattern to fax machines, beepers, cell phones, Internet access, e-mail, AOL, Wi-Fi access, smartphone Internet access—you name it. Some people were slow to adapt, but today, virtually everyone has access to the Internet in their pocket at all times. The Internet is available pretty much anywhere today, even on airplanes. (I'm still up in the air on whether Wi-Fi on a plane is a blessing or not. No pun intended.)

Marketing gets a customer through the door, but social media keeps them there and keeps the conversation going.

Too many brands confuse the two. They think social media is marketing. Social media is not a platform for you to sell your stuff. Social media is a platform for you to build a community, engage with that community, and become the go-to source for what you do. When you do that, people look to you as providing valuable, trusted, reliable resources to them. What does that do? It allows you to remain top of mind so when people are ready to make a buying decision, which is going to happen anyway, you are among their first choices. You eventually become an automatic, obvious choice. Doing business with you becomes an absolute no-brainer.

Do not get the two confused. Social media is, perhaps, a form of marketing because by using it you are indeed marketing yourself. But it is not your main advertising platform. You are not blasting your message and shoving it down consumers' throats. That is what advertising is for. Social media is here for you to explain your brand and tell your story—not to constantly pitch your brand. This does not mean that you can't sometimes promote your brand via social media. It just means that listening and engaging always comes first. This is where social media is most useful. Selling and pitching always comes second.

I like to say that the selling process is now the last process. Social media is more concerned with building the community, engaging with that community, and providing valuable content. As my buddy Joe Pulizzi of the Content Marketing Institute says, it is about providing "epic content marketing." In a nutshell, it simply means giving the people (your audience) what they want—giving them something of value that they can engage in, share, like and want more of. If people are sharing your message and content, all of a sudden they are marketing your information in addition to what you are already doing. That is really where the power of social media becomes crystal clear: when you're able to form a volunteer army of ambassadors who tell the story of your brand for you.

In his new book, appropriately titled *Epic Content Marketing*, Pulizzi says, "Good social media is preference related, and in most cases uninterested consumers can simply tune your message out." It is vital that people can connect with you almost instantaneously on Facebook, Twitter, your blog, your YouTube channel, or via any other social media venue. But if you are shoving your message down consumers' throats and constantly pushing instead of pulling them in and engaging them with valuable content, they can quickly tune you out.

> PRO TIP: Remember, consumers, prospects, and customers can tune you out just as quickly and easily as they can tune you in. Because social media is so preference related, you have got to be extremely careful. The last thing you want to do is have somebody tune you out because your message is overkill and constantly a "push" versus a "pull" effort.

Remember that if what you have to say is not relevant to what your audience wants and requests, they are not going to listen to you. They are going to tune you out. The bottom line is that you don't talk to people about something they don't want to hear. Think about what you want to read, the groups you join, the people you follow, the people you like, the people you engage with online. What if they started talking about the polar opposite of what they originally had started talking about? You would quickly tune them out, right? Prospects and existing customers will do the same to you if your message is not consistent and preference related.

Ask your customers what you are doing right and what you are doing wrong. Literally, ask them. They want to tell you. They want to be heard. Don't you? Listening is so underrated these days. Brands just don't want to listen. They think because Facebook has more than a billion users and Twitter has millions, those tools serve as giant megaphones. They think it is okay to blast a message and push, push, push, saying, "Here's my message, here's my message ..."

When you do that, you are not listening. You are only making noise and hoping people will listen, but they are actually doing quite the opposite. They are tuning you out and they are tuning you out at a rapid rate. They are simply clicking "Unfollow," "Unlike," "Hide," "Block," "Mute." There are tons of easy ways for people to tune you out instantaneously with the simple click of a mouse. Don't fall victim to that.

Listen to what people are telling you. Who is doing social media right? We all know Starbucks, the coffee shop on just about every corner. They are doing social media right. Why? Because they are not using social media to sell coffee. I know what you are thinking: "They don't need to sell coffee via social media because they're a billion-dollar corporation that sells coffee without even trying." But how do they continue to grow? They continue to grow by listening to their audience.

Starbucks launched a campaign called "Share. Vote. Discuss. See" not long ago that allowed them to request feedback from their existing customers. All they wanted to know was how they could improve their brand, their product, and their customer experience. They asked people to share their thoughts, to give them feedback. What did the campaign result in? Fifty-thousand brand-new product ideas for Starbucks. What did they do to get those 50,000 new ideas? They just asked, and after they asked, they just listened. Simple as that. You can read more details about that campaign here: http://bit.ly/SVDSStbks

Never underestimate the power of listening to your customers, and never underestimate the power of asking them what they want. Definitely never underestimate the power of paying attention to what they tell you, especially when they tell you exactly what they want. Do not let this idea go by the wayside. Ask them and listen carefully to what they say. Figure out precisely what they want and follow up by doing it. Social media is as much about listening as it is about talking. When you listen, you learn and you evolve.

Welcome to the Future, Kids!

Welcome to the future. We are living in one of the most exciting times ever. It's crazy to think that the tools and resources we use every single day—Facebook, Twitter, YouTube, blogs, and the numerous other social platforms—did not really exist in any significant way, with any sort of critical mass, in 2007. They were there, but masses of people were still skeptical about what the whole social media thing was really all about.

Today we can send information to a platform of more than a billion people in a matter of seconds. We can also target our message precisely, knowing exactly whom we want to talk to, and how and where we want to talk to them. We can engage with the people who really want to hear from us and avoid putting our message in front of people who do not want to see it.

Think about how ineffective junk mail used to be—straight from your mailbox to the trashcan without even being opened. Most of the time, those marketers had to send that same piece of mail with the same message on it seven or eight times before you would even look at it—and nine or ten times before you would even open it. How many times would it take for you to call that business, if you even did that at all, based on a piece of junk mail? How many pieces of junk mail would it take to get you to pick up the phone and inquire about whatever it was they were marketing?

◇◇

We no longer look for news and information; it comes directly to us.

◇◇

It comes via e-mail, Facebook, or our smart-phones. When most people wake up in the morning, even before they use the bathroom or make a pot of coffee, they check their Facebook page, and they check Twitter.

I depend on Twitter for news and information. Forget about turning on CNN, also known as Constant Negative News, when I can look on Twitter. Most traditional and major media outlets look to Twitter for breaking news first. We knew on Twitter that Osama bin Laden had been captured even before the news broke on CNN or the other traditional media outlets. If that is not powerful, I am not sure what is. Furthermore, *Yellow Pages*, roadside billboards, and television advertising campaigns are nearly obsolete. Few people look to these venues anymore. They are all looking down at their smartphones. These days, major media outlets have teams of people scouring Twitter and other real-time social media outlets for the most up-to-date, breaking news. Consumers alike are doing the same. It's a race to see who can break news first in the form of an online post.

Gary Vaynerchuk gave a talk, one time, about roadside billboards, asking why in the world you would invest in a roadside billboard ad. Do you think people are looking at your message? I think he said something like, "No, stupid, they're driving their car."

Traditional means of advertising are dead. Storytelling is the new way brands get their message out to the masses, and in my opinion will continue to be. Word of mouth is probably the best use of storytelling for brands. It consists of authentic, real-life case studies that influence someone's buying decisions based on the simple fact that they saw someone else make a similar decision, with a positive experience.

How about *Yellow Pages*? Well, my daughter's grown up now, but the only use I ever had for a *Yellow Pages* directory while she was growing up was as something she could sit on so she could reach the dinner table. Television advertising campaigns are nearly obsolete, too. How many times do you take full advantage of your DVR or TiVo while watching your favorite television show? When was the last time you actually watched a commercial, unless it was during the Super Bowl?

Let's talk about those Super Bowl commercials. Large brands spend millions of dollars for 30 to 60 seconds of airtime. Are commercials during the Super Bowl still very exciting and one of the most interesting elements of the Super Bowl viewing experience? Absolutely. But as you will see, despite the money spent and the large television audience, nine times out of ten, the commercial is only part of the strategy.

If the brand is smart, the television ad is connected to a call to action via social media. You will see a portion of the video, a portion of the television commercial during the Super Bowl, and it will tell you to like the brand on Facebook, follow it on Twitter, or check it out on YouTube. The overall message is completed when traditional media meet digital media and new media. This is where they intersect. I believe this is one of the most powerful concepts ever to take place in any media space.

Early in 2012, I was cast for a reality show on FOX TV. It was a one-off deal, for just a single show, but it was still an opportunity to be on FOX. Soon after getting cast, I had to fly to New York for the day to meet with the show's executives. I flew in early that morning. My interview was literally 10 or 15 minutes long and I was done for the day.

> **PRO TIP:** If you're marketing and advertising your brand via traditional media, be sure that you have a solid tie in with social media that will allow you to capture customers and get them into your ecosystem.

I had gotten into New York City at 10 a.m. My meeting would be 15 minutes long, tops, and I had the entire day to myself before my flight left at 6 p.m. Having only been to New York once before, for one day when I was young, I wanted to take full advantage of my short time there. I wanted to meet a friend for lunch and take in whatever sights I could.

As I walked through Times Square, I was like a kid in a candy store. I was absolutely fascinated by all of the nonstop action. But the thing that struck me the most was that I was standing in the advertising mecca of the world, where brands were spending millions upon millions of dollars to get their messages out to tourists and people who live there, every day, and no one was looking up at those messages. Where was everyone looking? They were looking down at their smartphones. Why? Because we no longer get our news and information from traditional outlets such as billboards and blinking signs.

News and information is coming directly to us. I found that extremely exciting and motivating, considering that I own a social media agency, but especially because I was looking down at my smartphone and ignoring all of the traditional advertising, just like everyone else.

I took a picture of Times Square and tweeted it. I shot some video and posted it and wrote, "Hey, I'm walking around Times Square, the advertising mecca of the world, yet no one's looking at the ads. They're looking down at their phones. I wonder why. Are they sending tweets?"

I wanted to document that moment in early 2011. I wanted to spread the word that traditional advertising does not offer the most relevant messages these days. It is not where all of the eyeballs are. Are any eyeballs still on it at all? Yes, but I believe there are a lot more eyes on the digital space than on the traditional space. This should serve as evidence of the rapid rate at which we receive information today. No matter what you are trying to do with social media, you have to meet people where they are. You have to be where the eyeballs are.

A lot of people say to me, "I don't think I'm ready for social media yet. I don't see the return on investment for social media. I don't know why my brand should be social." The first thing I say to them is, "Social media is where the eyeballs are." That is where all advertisers and marketers want to put their message, where the eyeballs are.

Why some people still do not understand that is beyond me, but it is not my job to sell them and convince them on that idea.

I often go back to a quote from my friend Gary Vaynerchuk:

"Social media is overthrowing governments in the Middle East. Do you really have the audacity to think it's not affecting your business?" – Gary Vaynerchuk

I think he absolutely nails it with that statement. I have quoted that statement in my e-mail signature. I repeat it constantly, and I quote it regularly, because it is so accurate and so difficult to argue with.

You cannot argue the fact that governments are being overthrown in the Middle East because of social media. It is happening. If such huge, monumental events like that are taking place, how in the world could social media not be affecting your brand? The next time you think social media may or may not be for your brand, consider that statement.

Of course, you are probably interested in social media, and you believe in the power of it, because you are reading this book. We can connect with the world instantly and thus spread our message far and wide in the time it takes to click a mouse or hit "Send." That is so powerful. How do we manage all of this potential? You will need to keep reading to find out. The answers are here.

Want to Be Remembered? Keep It Simple

Here is the story I heard about how Nike came up with its "Just do it" slogan and advertising campaign. The Nike executive advertising team was in a meeting with its ad agency discussing the previous advertising campaign, which had just run and had been successful. As the discussion continued, someone from the ad agency looked at the team of Nike execs and said, "Man, you guys just do it." In that very moment, over a simple conversation about ending Nike's previous advertising campaign and starting a new one, they coined what is now probably one of the most prevalent and memorable marketing campaigns ever. I can't think of too many advertising slogans that are more recognizable than "Just Do It," can you? There may be a few, but that one is way up there.

Not only was the phrase utilized in advertising, it is now utilized in everyday life. It is just something we say now. When you are encouraging someone, when you are thinking about something that you need to do and you are finding a tough time getting to it, what is the first thing that comes to mind? "Just Do It." The same applies to being able to create a message for your brand. Once you come up with a consistent message or phrase pertaining to your brand, it is hard to let go of that. So make sure it is a message that you are comfortable being associated with for a long time should it catch on, as "Just do it" has.

Check out the mini case study on how "Just Do It" was coined by Nike at: http://bit.ly/NikeJDI.

The bow tie is marketable. People are attracted to it. People look at me every time they see me, and instead of calling me Sebastian, they say, "Social Buzz," or "the Bow Tie Guy." I could not escape these words even if I tried.

With very large advertising campaigns, nine times out of ten, the message is very simple. Barack Obama's 2008 presidential campaign was probably one of the most brilliantly conceived and executed campaigns ever. Why? It was simple. It was motivating and easy to digest. My buddy Bruce Turkel thinks the "Yes, We Can" campaign is, hands down, one of the largest, most successful advertising campaigns to date: "Yes" — it's positive. "We" — it's inclusive. "Can" — it's aspirational.

Look at McDonald's. Whether you like the food or not, the company has had some very creative advertising and marketing campaigns. One that comes to mind right off the bat is "I'm Lovin' It." McDonald's—I'm lovin' it. How about the competition, Burger

WANT TO BE REMEMBERED? KEEP IT SIMPLE

King? People refer to the very effective slogan when they jokingly say, "Hey, this isn't Burger King." If you remember, Burger King had great success with the "Your Way Right Away" campaign (and before that, "Have It Your Way"). They were basically saying, "When you walk in and tell us what kind of burger you want, you're able to have it your way right away." It is very important for a brand to be able to describe itself in very few words.

My friend Bruce Turkel constantly points out that brands are not about an individual. He says, "Your brand is not about you," which is true. Your brand is not about you. He follows that up with, "Your brand is about what your product or service does for someone else. More importantly, it's about how your product or service makes them feel."

Bruce also gets to the essence of branding. He says, "A good brand makes you feel good. A great brand makes you feel good about yourself." I could not agree more. Good brands make you feel good. Great brands make people feel good about themselves. When you are able to make people feel good about themselves and connect that feeling to your brand, you have a lifelong customer. Why? Because your product, brand, or service caters to them, makes them feel good, and fulfills a solution. It creates nothing but good feelings and most of us respond to good feelings.

Nike's "Just Do It" campaign allows you to associate with a large brand. You wear the brand's shoes and clothes, and every time you see that Nike swoosh, the first thing that comes to mind is "Just Do It." The brand taps into the emotional side of you, the consumer. "Just Do It" is a bold and powerful phrase, a very positive phrase. And by association, when you utilize Nike products, that phrase applies to you. Nikes makes you feel good about yourself. That is an example of a great brand.

Before that slogan was born, Nike was competing against archrival Reebok. Post-slogan, in the 1990s, Nike rose about as fast and high as any company possibly could. With its slogan, iconic swoosh, and sports megastars such as Michael Jordan as spokespeople, the Nike brand adopted a new religion of brand consciousness, managing to be both anti-establishment and mass market.

In 1997, Nike posted $9.2 billion in sales. In the 1980s and 1990s, traditional advertising turned huge profits for companies such as Nike. Today, those strategies and those messages are communicated via social media. It is all about image and perception. Marketing grabs the customer's attention, and social media keeps the conversation going. The messages of large brands have not changed much, but now they are easier to convey to a larger audience because of the tools we have available to us.

Take Twitter, for example. Gary Vaynerchuk says Twitter is the most powerful website on the planet. I believe that wholeheartedly. Twitter is the new telephone. Even Twitter branded itself with a very short and simple message that proved to be extremely effective: "Twitter: Join the Conversation." I use that phrase when people ask me what Twitter is all about. I tell them it is the most powerful website on the planet and it allows people to do just what its slogan says: join the conversation. Speaking of Gary and of Nike, I remember him giving a prediction one time of how large brands will market to their target demographic in the very near future, He said brands like Nike will read a tweet or social media post from you that may include something like "I'm going for a run" – the next day you will have a knock on your door with a delivery of six pairs of brand new NIKE running shoes. It will blow your mind and you will by default become a loyal fan of NIKE. Not only do you win, but NIKE wins because it's cheaper for them to target conversations of people within their target demographic than it would be to spend large ad dollars to attempt to find you.

Here's a clip of Gary sharing this from his 2010 book tour stop in Miami: http://bit.ly/GaryVNikeStory.

Twitter is a professional conversation that is happening 365 days a year, 24 hours a day, 7 days a week. It never stops. It is a fire hose of information—news information, community and the ability to connect with any single person you want to connect with. That is branding: being able to tell people exactly what you are doing with your brand, joining the conversation.

So, those slogans, those messages by Nike, Burger King, McDonald's, and Obama's 2008 presidential campaign are all things of the past. But the common denominator is that they are all still relevant messages ingrained in our minds. We remember them, and they are part of our lives. Twitter, founded in 2006, came up with a short, highly effective message: "Join the conversation." You want to do the same for your brand. Keep it short and simple, and ask yourself. "Will people remember this 25 years from now?"

> **PRO TIP:** If your message is something that resonates with people, if it offers them something or makes them feel good, it is going to be ingrained in their minds. They will share it with other people. They will remember it forever.

This is why brands like Nike, McDonald's, Burger King, and the presidential race of 2008 remain top of mind even though the ship has sailed on these marketing campaigns. They will never be forgotten.

As long as we are talking about fast food, we have to include Wendy's. Who could forget the brilliance of the chain's visionary leader, Dave Thomas? I remember the Wendy's campaign of the 1980s as if it were yesterday. When I was a kid, I liked to mimic the commercial every time I walked into a Wendy's. I would peek over the counter and say, "Where's the beef?" Everyone remembers that campaign because it was simple, relevant, short, and sweet.

The "Where's the Beef?" campaign was Wendy's way of proving that it offered a significantly larger amount of meat per sandwich than its competitors did. When consumers were making buying decisions, thinking about which fast-food drive-through to go to, they remembered "Where's the Beef?" and then said to themselves, "Oh, I'm going to get more bang for my buck if I go to Wendy's instead of Burger King or McDonald's. Why? Wendy's is giving me more beef." Wendy's stayed top of mind.

It was an effective and memorable slogan that gave people something useful and of value, and it made them feel good about themselves and their decision to give their business to Wendy's. The best part is it consisted of a grand total of three words.

When you come up with a simple, effective way to brand yourself and you convey a message that tells people your brand is doing something for them—something that makes them feel good—you ingrain yourself in their minds and they never, ever forget about you.

So, when I thought about what history has taught us over the past 25 years, with brands conceptualizing short, effective advertising slogans and messages, I had a light bulb moment and came up with this key question: Was all of that leading us to where we are today with social media? I think the answer is yes.

"Just Do It," "Where's the Beef?" "I'm Lovin' It," "Your Way Right Away"—all of these short, effective, memorable messages have led us straight to where we are right now with social media. Because what does social media really do? How does it operate? Twitter gives us the ability to convey our messages to the masses in 140 characters or less, and Facebook lets us do the same by posting a picture with one sentence attached to it.

Now let me be clear. I do not believe any of this new technology will replace large-scale advertising and marketing campaigns. It's not going to replace television commercials, glossy print ads, or major-event sponsorships any time soon. I just believe that large brands are rethinking how their message is going to be conveyed. They are realizing that this new technology, this new way of communicating to the masses, is a perfect fit for what they have been doing for the past 25 years, and even back beyond that. Social media allows them to continue to do what they have always done: come up with a short, effective message that will reach the masses and, most importantly, stick with the masses and tell the brand's story.

Let's look at the delivery service industry: Fed Ex and UPS. I spoke once at a branding seminar. The head creative guy there was the art director for the great Dunkin' Donuts campaign, "Time to Make the Donuts." He had come up with that great, unforgettable slogan. We all remember the commercial of the short guy with the mustache who would wake up in the middle of the night and, half asleep, say "Time to make the donuts." Well, the guy who came up with that was also the head of the FedEx advertising and marketing campaign back in the 1980s when Federal Express started flying everywhere. The company started running those ads with the tagline, "When it absolutely positively has to be there overnight." They were Federal Express back then. They even shortened the name of the company, further proof that brevity is powerful!

UPS was not advertising as strongly as FedEx was, primarily because FedEx was going through a transition at the time. FedEx was now flying and offering overnight delivery, as opposed to its previous model of ground delivery only. The campaign consisted of a series of very comical conversations about this package or that package not arriving when it needed to arrive.

It constantly kept the FedEx brand top of mind. When you knew that you needed to get a package somewhere overnight, Federal Express was your obvious choice. The message was a little bit longer than "Just Do It," but every time you saw it, you were reminded of this simple fact: "If you need to get a package someplace tomorrow, guaranteed, you need to ship it via FedEx." We automatically associated that brand and its reliability with that message: "When it absolutely, positively has to be there overnight." It made FedEx the go-to resource in its field.

All of the major delivery services of today—FedEx, UPS, DHL— have come up with creative, catchy phrases to help brand themselves in what has become the highly competitive market of international delivery services. UPS says, "We run the tightest ship in the shipping business," and DHL says, "We move the world." These three brands dominate the industry, but FedEx led the way and continues to do so. Again, you have to give the company credit for taking it all the way and even shortening its name. FedEx is much catchier and more memorable than Federal Express, both when you hear it and when you see it. And how about UPS? Much more memorable than United Parcel Service, don't you think?

Both FedEx and UPS have simplified their messages, too. FedEx went from "When it absolutely, positively has to be there overnight" to "The world on time." In addition to UPS's, "We run the tightest ship in the shipping business," the company posed a rhetorical question:

"What can Brown do for you?" This plays on the company's signature color, further branding itself and keeping itself top of mind.

It is very important to realize that your brand message may start out a little bit longer than it eventually becomes as your brand evolves. Your goal is always to ingrain your message in people's consciousness. The name of my company, my brand, is SocialBuzzTV. com. Everyone and his mother refers to me as Social Buzz. That is awesome, not only because people remember me and keep me top of mind, but also because most of my brand name, the most important part of it, is what people say out loud, over and over: Social Buzz.

Why Word of Mouth Counts and Always Has

In my opinion, social media has put a tremendous amount of horsepower behind word of mouth. Seeing that we connect instantly these days, we no longer have to call, write, or visit people to get their opinion on something we may want or need. We see it by default on Facebook or Twitter. Gary Vaynerchuk said it best: "Word-of-mouth has never gone away. It's just scalable these days." Today word-of-mouth marketing is amplified to the tenth degree by social media. Few things are more valuable to a business than a positive referral. We all want to be endorsed, and we all want a good recommendation when it is time for us to make a purchase.

Peer recommendations are far more effective in this day and age than any advertising campaign would ever be. Does that mean advertising is irrelevant? No. Does that mean marketing campaigns are irrelevant? No. Marketing and advertising campaigns keep the message fresh in our minds and social media keeps the conversation going. But peer recommendations are key. When somebody close to us—somebody we know, like and trust—is endorsing a product, service or brand, it often becomes the single, most-valuable piece of information we consider in our buying decisions. Why? We know somebody who has already experienced that product or service. They have tested it. They trust the brand and we trust them. That is all we usually need. It's the old "If it's good enough for him, it's good enough for me" mentality.

Word of mouth has always been around, but today, it is scalable. If people say, "Sebastian, I'm looking for a good mechanic in Miami," and I've got a client or buddy who is a mechanic and whom I can recommend, all I have to do is tag that person on Facebook or Twitter and do an introduction via Facebook or e-mail.

Word of mouth has never been more prevalent or spread more easily. Why? Because of the tools and resources social media offers us to make spreading the word and/or making recommendations simple. That is what makes word of mouth so effective these days. We can tag someone, tweet someone, post something on some-body's wall, send a message, and instantaneously connect. This is yet another *vital* reason that brands need to leverage the power of social media. If you're not there, they can't find you. Even worse, they can't recommend you.

Word of mouth is also scalable if there has been a positive or negative experience with a brand. When I have a not-so-awesome dining experience at a local restaurant (and, thankfully, that does not happen very often), the first thing I do is hit up the restaurant directly. If I don't get a response from the manager, I take it public via Twitter and Facebook to try and find out if anybody else has had a similar experience.

At home, I use a particular cable television company that I will not mention. Every time I am frustrated with the company (and sadly this happens very often), I write, "This cable company sucks," on Twitter. Almost instantaneously, I get contacted by someone from the customer service department asking how the company can resolve the issue. I am asked to direct-message (DM) my private contact information to the company via Twitter so someone can address my problem. Almost every time, I get a phone call from the corporate office asking what the problem is and how the company can best resolve it.

Although I really despise this local cable company, it is the only provider in the area, so I have no choice other than to give up Internet access and cable television. So, I continue to put up with it. But I do have to give it to the company for being able to utilize and leverage social media and understand that word of mouth, even in a negative space, is something it uses to its advantage. The company can correct its (many!) mistakes via social media.

Google and Bing also do a good job of making word of mouth scalable. In the past, consumers made choices based on the first or biggest or fanciest advertisement they noticed in the *Yellow Pages* directory. *Yellow Pages*? Wait a minute! Do they even make those anymore? *Yellow Pages* directories were a slightly random way of selecting goods and services. Today, the best use of a *Yellow Pages* directory is as a door stop. Google, Bing, and Facebook know more about us than most online entities do. And that is a good thing. We want them to know as much about us as possible. We want them to know our preferences so that we mostly see the things we want to see and we do not see the things that are of no interest to us. Just about the only thing you should conceal from Google, Bing, and Facebook is your Social Security number and banking information. Other than that, let them in. Let them know what you like. Let them know how you live. Let them know what you are looking for. This is our reality today. This is how we receive information.

> **PRO TIP:** If you are a business owner and someone complains about your brand online, it is *imperative* that you respond quickly and decisively. Defend your brand, or else word of mouth will spread the wrong message. You cannot stop the flow of word of mouth, but you can influence the message being spread.

Word of mouth is as strong and popular as it ever has been. Social media outlets add a new component to word of mouth: scalability. Think about it. Fifteen years ago, the media would publish bad news about a company if the brand were relevant enough and made enough negative noise. But these days, brands can be slaughtered by the public in a matter of seconds, and the viral effect is even scarier. Word to the wise brand: *always* do the right thing. Nothing will ever be perfect, and mistakes will happen. But it's how your brand responds that will soften the blow of any mistake.

Word of mouth is essential, the same way it was in the 1950s when it spread through an entire town if a customer had a bad experience with a local business. The only difference today is that word of mouth reaches more people almost instantaneously because of social media.

Am I saying that every time you have a bad experience at a restaurant you should make sure to send a message out on Twitter? I would. Why not? It's important that (A) you get your bad experience corrected, and (B) the venue be notified about any unsatisfied customers so it can assure the situation is rectified before the conversation escalates.

I don't know about sending out a mass message on social media every single time, but you definitely should contact the brand every time for the reasons I mentioned above. In the event that you do not get a response from the brand, it is your prerogative to talk about it publicly on social media. Either way, it is all about getting the conversation going, whether it is negative or positive.

It is my belief that brands, especially large brands, are now starting to wake up and realize even more that people are talking about them online whether they like it or not. Sometimes the talk is negative. Sometimes it is positive. But the bottom line is that people are talking about them.

One of the biggest mistakes brands make today is avoiding social media for fear of it becoming a complaint box. They think, "If I have these platforms set up, people are going to say something negative about me." I have news for brand managers who think like that: people are already talking about their company. But if those brands engage in social media, they will have a platform that enables them to play defense, to turn negatives into positives through clear communication and attentive customer service. Think about my cable company. I despise it and think it does a horrible job, yet I have given it credit for at least trying to make things better. The conversations I have with that company's representatives when I have problems prove that the company cares, even if it is incompetent.

Some people say, "We got negative feedback on our Yelp page [or our website], so we just deleted it." I will *never* understand that madness. That is probably one of the most insane things a brand could ever possibly do. What a great way to poke the bear, to make the customer who is already upset even more upset. Now he is going to come back and comment again on not only the initial problem, but also the added problem of being ignored and brushed out the back door.

What is the best course of action, then, if someone is completely raking your brand over the coals by saying something negative? I will tell you. The best course of action is to face the music. "Brand up" and ask the customer what went wrong. Ask customers about their negative experience. Give them an opportunity to vent. People just want to be heard. After they have gotten it all out, ask them what you can do to make things right. This is just simple customer service protocol, nothing new for smart brands. But now that customer service and word of mouth are scalable, it is absolutely vital that every business, large or small, take care of its upset customers.

At the same time, it is also very important that you take care of a customer who is saying positive things about you. A simple thank-you or some kind of follow-up can allow you to take a positive situation and make it even better. We all want to be heard when we have a problem, but we also want to be acknowledged when we compliment or do business with a brand.

Think about the times you have interacted with a brand and had a positive experience. You cannot wait to tell somebody about it. What is the first thing you do if someone asks you about that brand? You sing its praises and tell that person how well the brand treated you. That is the type of brand you want to be. For most of us, it is in our nature to pass along the good word. We want good things to happen to us and when they do, we want to share the experience.

In Gary Vaynerchuk's second book, *The Thank-You Economy*, he talks about a case study of AJ Bombers, a hamburger joint in Milwaukee, Wisconsin. When AJ Bombers first opened, it allowed its customers to be part of the menu experience, to actually help create the menu. AJ Bombers asked its customers what they liked. Some customers were even able to design specific burgers that are now on today's menu.

One day, the restaurant had to shut down the kitchen for a few hours while some work was done. Instead of just telling people the restaurant was closed, the managers put a video screen outside, in front of the business, streaming a live, upstream video of the work being done in the kitchen for the customers to see. They could have just put up a sign reading, "Closed for repairs," or something like that. But instead, they interacted with their customers and showed them that they were not just going through the motions. They wanted to show their customers that they weren't pleased that the customers could not come in for a bite to eat. They also provided free beer and peanuts while the repairs were being done.

Another way the restaurant managers turned negatives into positives was early on when they received negative feedback from a few customers, either about the food or the service. They invited those customers back again and again until their negative experiences turned positive. Sometimes, the customers would come back four or five times until they were happy. But when you do something like that, when you put forth that kind of effort to right your wrongs, once that customer is happy, you have got that customer for life. You have shown that you are committed to taking that customer from a negative space into a positive space. That is vitally powerful. Never underestimate the value of taking an upset customer and turning that person into a satisfied customer and raving fan.

I like to tell the story of how I made the foolish decision of switching from an iPhone to an Android. I went into the AT&T store and the salesman told me he had the most-cutting-edge technology for this new Android device. I had been an iPhone guy ever since I put down the BlackBerry and realized that smartphones were where it was at. But I thought maybe it was time for something new. So I went ahead and upgraded—I don't know if I would call it an upgrade, it was more of a downgrade—to this new Android phone that I had bought online. I renewed my contract. I got the phone.

It was horrible. Every single day, the phone would freeze. I had to constantly take the battery out. The battery life seemed to last maybe five minutes, if that. I was extremely frustrated with what they called the Android platform. I wanted my iPhone back. Maybe more than that, I wanted to just give the Android back before I ran it over with my car. After constant arguing with AT&T representatives, who kept reminding me that all sales were final and nothing was going to change, and that they were sorry but that was the way it was, I decided to write a blog post titled "AT&T Sucks." I tweeted it and posted it everywhere. I was approached by an AT&T representative, who asked me what the biggest challenge was. I told him that I had renewed my contract and switched from the iPhone to the Android platform, which was, hands-down, one of the biggest mistakes of my life. I said I just wanted to give the Android back and get an iPhone.

After continued resistance, and hearing the representative say over and over that the company could not do anything for me, he finally called me back a week or so later and said, "Hey, Mr. Rusk, we were able to find a refurbished iPhone 4. For your troubles, we're going to

FedEx it to you free of charge and give you the phone as well. Will that satisfy the challenge you had with us?"

I was kind of at a loss for words because (A) I was getting what I wanted, and most importantly, (B) a brand had listened to my concern and addressed it. I gladly accepted the offer. I took the Android phone and sold it on a website called Gazelle, which is, by the way, an awesome website.

You can sell used electronics on Gazelle for almost top dollar. Follow this link, http://bit.ly/GazelleLink to learn more about this service!

I ended up winning there. Even though I had switched from iPhone to Android—a huge mistake on my part—I ended up switching back to iPhone because I had complained enough. Does this mean that if you do not like something, as long as you get out there and complain, you will get something for free? No. But I had a legitimate concern. I had spent a couple hundred dollars on a brand-new Android phone. I was completely unsatisfied with it. I was locked into a contract and I just wanted AT&T to make it right. AT&T didn't lose a customer and I got the phone I preferred. It was a total "win-win" in my book. It took AT&T a while, but the company finally did just that: it heard my complaint, addressed it, and made things right. It turned into a win for me, and a win for AT&T too.

To be fair, I have got to give credit where credit is due. The Android platform has grown exponentially over the past few years. The company now makes a dynamite product, but my problem dates back a few years when it was just getting started and working all of the kinks out. But again, we are not talking specifically about smartphones here. I am just trying to offer an example of really effective customer service and really effective word of mouth. There are numerous other case studies, I'm sure, of brands that have connected with customers by means of social media, both positively and negatively.

Was my complaining going to put AT&T out of business? Probably not. But had AT&T not addressed my problem and had I continued to write negative things about the company, someone would have stumbled upon my blog posts and thought twice about doing business with AT&T, whether that person knew me or not.

As far as actual word of mouth goes, because I tell this story all the time, I guarantee you that people take my experience into consideration when they need to upgrade their phone. They think about the problems I had, but they also consider the fact that AT&T came through and actually made it right and corrected the situation. It was not an instantaneous "Let's make this better" by AT&T, but eventually that company came around. With the Milwaukee restaurant, AJ Bombers, it was an instantaneous "Let's make it better" and let's spend as much time and effort as we need to make it better. With AT&T it was, "Okay, we have decided to make it better after all." So better late than never, and it all got passed on through word of mouth, through stories that people communicate verbally or via social media.

Social media is a platform for us to build a community, engage with a community, and get our message out. But it is also a platform for managing and overseeing word of mouth. It is a platform for us to influence what is being said about us, correct our "wrongs," and acknowledge praise for our "rights." You have got to take the good with the bad. You have got to make the bad right and take the good and make it even better.

In the fall of 2013, I attended and covered the Pivot Conference in New York with my buddy Brian Solis. I decided to utilize the online platform Airbnb.com to find a place to stay as an alternative to a hotel. Airbnb.com is a great resource. You can use it to rent a room, rent a couch, or rent an entire house—whatever you need—and most of the time it is more cost effective than staying in a hotel. It's very user friendly. All of the places have been checked out and prescreened. You get pictures. You get reviews. You get people commenting about their experiences.

So, I decided to rent a room since I was going to be in New York City for four days. I decided to stay in Brooklyn. I had heard a lot of cool things about Brooklyn and knew it was not too far outside the city. So I found a place. The guy who was offering the room was really friendly. He said the view from the rooftop of his building was great, and that it was about a 20-minute ride into Manhattan. I thought, "Awesome. This sounds like a perfect fit for me."

I arrived that Sunday morning at JFK with my luggage. I had trouble finding the transit system to get me out of the airport and onto the subway. And when you are hefting bags, the scenic route around JFK is not the one you want to be on. So I finally made my way onto the actual subway and after about three stops, the train broke down. More importantly, there was a police investigation going on. I thought, "Wow, welcome to New York City."

I got off the subway, hopped in a cab, and quickly made it to Brooklyn. As I got out of the cab, I thought, "Um, this doesn't really look like the place online." A lot of us have had this experience with hotels. When I met the host, he immediately apologized and explained he had guests who had stayed in the room the previous night. "Guests" actually referred to a rock band that was staying there and just sort of hanging out and doing what rock bands do. It looked as if there had been an all-night party that was still going on and didn't seem to be going anywhere.

All I wanted to do was drop my bags because, at noon, I was headed to Hillsong New York City, a church I had long wanted to visit, and it was already nearing 11 a.m. The host said, "You can leave your stuff right here." I looked around at this rock band sitting there, looking as if they hadn't slept in days, and thought, "I'm not leaving my stuff here. There's no way."

So I took my bags and told the host I would be back later. He said he was working with Airbnb to get the guests out. He apologized profusely. I went to the city with my bags in tow. I went to the church. When I was done with the church, I decided I would not be staying in Brooklyn with the rock band. I knew I needed to get a hotel in Manhattan, which was where my event was going to be anyway.

I pulled up a hotel app called Hotel Tonight and found a room for a stellar rate. I booked the room immediately. The Brooklyn host told me that if I wanted to cancel the room at his place and get a refund, he would do whatever he could to make that happen. He contacted Airbnb to facilitate the cancellation and make sure I got a refund, including all fees that were charged to me from Airbnb for the booking.

Airbnb quickly got back to me and apologized extensively for my experience. They let me know that a refund had been processed immediately and would show up on my credit card within a couple of days.

I was ecstatic. I had found a great deal on a hotel smack dab in the middle of Times Square. I had received a refund for a not-so-awesome room that I thought was going to be great. But most importantly, Airbnb's customer service was completely impeccable on top of it. I do not know if I got lucky that one day or if Airbnb's customer service is that awesome all the time. I am going to assume the latter, because the story doesn't end there.

The next day, I woke up to an e-mail containing a Giftly.com gift certificate for $50. It was from my friends at Airbnb. They again apologized profusely for my experience and sent me a $50 gift certificate, saying, "Go have dinner on us." That is a phenomenal example of a brand going above and beyond what it already had done. I was already okay with the fact that the company had apologized. I was already okay with the fact that it had given me a refund, including all of the fees the company normally charged. I was ecstatic that I had found a room smack dab in the middle of Times Square. Then Airbnb went above and beyond and bought me dinner. Minus that early misstep, the experience could not have better.

Will I use Airbnb.com again? Absolutely. Will I tell my friends and family about my great experience and recommend Airbnb to them? Absolutely. I will tell them to make sure to do their due diligence and know exactly where they are staying and what the reality of the place is. But chances are things are going to work out whatever they choose, because Airbnb will make sure of it through the most effective real-time marketing. Well done, Airbnb.com. Well done!

Remember, word of mouth is something that has always been around. There were no fax machines. There were no social media platforms back then. It was just people talking to people. People either complained to one another or got excited about a brand and praised it to each other. Either way, people responded because that is part of our human nature.

We listen to other consumers because we often feel as if we are all in this together—us against them. We say, "Wait a second. If I shop there and my neighbor had a negative experience there, what's to say that I'm not going to have a negative experience there, too?" Or we say, "Well, my neighbor had a bad experience at Bob's Butcher Shop but Bob made it right by giving my neighbor a free batch of meat, and then offered everybody free samples of a new product." As long as you and your brand make an effort to make things better, people will usually forgive you. That is part of human nature, too.

> **PRO TIP: The best brands understand that word of mouth counts. They understand that it has always been around, but that, today, it is everywhere all at once.**

Never underestimate the power and influence of someone talking about your brand, positively or negatively. If you think you can hide from people on social media, you have got another think coming. Hiding from people on social media is just ignoring the inevitable. People are going to talk about you. It is your choice to respond or not, to make a negative situation positive, or to thank them when they tell you about a positive experience. Everyone likes to be thanked. Everyone likes to be heard. Everyone likes to get problems resolved, especially when it involves a consumer situation and a brand that can do something about it.

Don't give people a reason to talk badly about you or your brand. If they do, face the music. Let them vent. Let them tell you what went wrong and why they are upset. Once they do that, you will have an opportunity to go in and make it right. You are grossly negligent, as a brand manager/owner, if you ignore customers who are trying to praise your brand or complain about your brand. It's your job to make it right! You cannot make everyone happy. But there is a tremendous amount of opportunity in social media to fix things and open new doors, to turn negatives into positives, and reinforce positives with a simple thank-you. Good feelings equate to good business. And social media leads the way where good business is concerned.

Why Social Media Is No Longer a "Should" but a "Must"

Tony Robbins talks a lot about "shoulds." He says people are constantly saying to him, "You know, Tony, I should do this, and I should do that," and they find themselves "shoulding" all over themselves. The reality of participating in social media is that there is no more "should." It is an absolute "must." There are more than a billion people on social media, not to mention the brands that are leveraging the wide range of audiences on social media.

First of all, "should" is a fairly bad idea in most areas. Too much "shoulding" and that is what your whole life becomes—one big "should," and nothing meaningful or valuable ever gets done. "Should" applied to social media maybe five or six years ago: "We should be engaging in social media on behalf of our business but we're not doing it yet." It was kind of like, "We know we should eat broccoli because it's good for us but we don't eat it very often because we don't like the taste."

The option of making your brand social or not no longer exists. Social media is now a "must"—no longer a "should," even for the businesses most hesitant to adopt it. In 2014, your customers expect that you will engage in lively social media the same way they expected you to have a website at the turn of the 21st century and a telephone in 1954. Social media is becoming a normal, essential part of doing business every single day. The brands that still have not adopted social media are missing out on new customers, interaction with existing customers and full-scale business opportunities. Period.

Among other things, social media is how customers give businesses feedback, good or bad, and how businesses respond to feedback. It is a new avenue of communication for a brand's customer service program. In the last chapter, we talked about customer service and word of mouth. Social media is the absolute lifeblood of your brand's customer service capabilities. It allows customers to give you feedback. It allows you to hear the feedback, respond to it, and constantly refine your brand and improve your customer experience. Again, social media is not a "should"; it is a "must." Social media also allows your customers to communicate with you via a different route. It's the 21st century, and no one wants to pick up the phone to complain anymore. That's so 1995.

Let's talk a little bit more about why social media is a "must." Some businesses are afraid of social media, because they see it as a vehicle for exposing negative aspects of their brand. Would you ever say to yourself, "You know, I shouldn't offer customer service to my customers" No, you absolutely would not say that. That would be brand suicide, because as the old quote reads, "If you don't take care of your customers, someone else will!" Some brands are still hiding in the shadows because they think social media interaction puts them in the spotlight in a bad way. I hear a lot about this. People say, "I don't want to utilize social media because people are just going to talk badly about me."

Here is how I respond to that. The first thing I ask is why people are talking badly about your brand. You're probably giving them a reason to do so. That may be the first issue you want to correct. Second, even if you hide from them, they'll talk about you anyway. They could have their own blog. They could have their own business. They could tweet, post, post a video on YouTube, share comments on additional blog posts, and worse yet, share comments on your competition's blog posts. Guess what, friends? If you think people will talk about your brand only if you have a social media site, you have another thing coming: they are already talking about you.

Gary Vaynerchuk says, "Do you care about what people are saying about your brand? You'd better." The train keeps rolling. Why not get on board and participate in the conversation? The train is not slowing down and it is definitely not stopping. You either get on it, or your customers will be on it along with your competition, all of them rolling away from you, at a rapid speed.

If a company is so worried about the negativity that social media would bring to its brand, I would encourage that company to reevaluate how it does business and represents itself. Period. If you are representing yourself in a negative manner, it is no mystery why people are talking about you in a negative context. If your customers have had a negative experience with your product, brand, service, or all of the above, and you have not responded accordingly, it is your fault. If you have not figured out a way to make things right, to make that customer go from unhappy to happy, it is your fault. Your customers should not be talking negatively about you. However, if you are operating in a positive manner, making sure you are listening, responding and engaging with them—taking them from unhappy to happy or happy to happier—then congrats, you are doing your job.

It is not always going to be perfect and it is not always going to be easy.

> PRO TIP: You can't please everyone, as the old saying always goes, but with social media you can definitely take customers from unhappy to happy by simply listening to their concerns. It is everywhere all at once.

You can also take customers from happy to happier by thanking them and telling them how much you appreciate the fact that they engage with you and do business with you. Remember that when a customer makes a buying decision in your favor, it is not because they're thinking, "I 'should' buy this product or service." Instead, they're thinking, "I 'must' buy this product because I want to." The same applies to your brand. You use social media as a means of customer service because you want to and you have to—not because you should.

Social media is not a fast track for sales. In fact, sales is the last step in the process when it comes to social media. Social media puts you on the fast track to credibility, to becoming the go-to source for what you do in your community. Social media is, quite simply, the place for you to tell your story, for your network to tell their version of your story, for dialogue to occur between you and your customers. This includes feedback, and questions and answers in both directions.

When I launched SocialBuzzTV.com, I wanted to build a sustainable brand that people would want to invest in long-term. I also wanted to help people discover and understand what they didn't know about social media. Back in 2005, social media was the Wild Wild West. People thought you were an absolute maniac if you were on MySpace, exposing your life to the world. "Why in the world would you ever want to do that?" they would say. I did not think that way. I thought of MySpace as more of an online high school reunion. You could connect with people you wanted to connect with and sometimes people came out of the woodwork, people you did not want to connect with. But, overall, it was good. As the social space continued to grow and Facebook evolved, more and more people got involved. Soon, social media became a big part of the normal way we communicated with each other.

As people started to adapt to social media more and more, I started to think about helping them to better understand the hows and whys. There would be a tremendous amount of value in that. If I produced content on the relevancy of social media, it would sink in. If I built my brand, told my story about how I built it from nothing other than social media, I knew that would sink in too. Those ideas would open people's eyes and help them better understand exactly what social media was all about. More importantly, those concepts would keep me top of mind with people and, by default, make me their go-to source when it came to social media.

I hear that all the time. "We love your work. We love what you're doing. We'd love to sit down and talk with you. We hear you're the best." I don't necessarily know if I agree with that statement, because there is always somebody better out there. But the bottom line is, people contact me and give me positive feedback about what I'm doing and how I am managing my brand.

I often share my story with people. I tell them how I came from nothing to where I am now. I had lost it all, I was frustrated, and I subsequently built this brand with social media exclusively. Thankfully, these platforms are free and all I had to do was be consistent and diligent in my efforts. I only had to create and push out content daily. Now I have a sustainable brand that people believe in and I have become a go-to source for them when it comes to social media.

There was a point in time when people did not realize they needed a telephone until a telephone was readily available. When the telephone became more prevalent, everyone wanted a telephone. Every household had a telephone, every business started to have a telephone, and then every corner started to have payphones. Then what happened? Life without telephones became unimaginable. After telephones, came fax machines and beepers. Next came cell phones, and then smartphones. Now we, basically, have instantaneous communication at our fingertips. That is where we are today with social media. We could not imagine going back to prior technology or prior realities. Whether you want to admit it or not, we are digitally addicted.

Beside all of its business ramifications, social media allows us to keep in touch with people who live far from us, including, of course, our closest friends and family. It is the new telephone call, letter, slide show, and home-movie session all wrapped into one. If you have any argument against that, please see YouTube.com for confirmation. More than 70 hours of video are uploaded to YouTube every minute. That's crazy.

Every means of communication technology that has helped improve our lives was at one time on the fringe and largely not adopted. All of it went from being a "should" to a "must." Again, this is where we are with social media today, right on that cusp. Too many people still underestimate the power of social media. It is still in its infancy. But make no mistake. It is alive and well. Social media may be an infant but it is a healthy, growing infant, 100 percent alive. That excites me to no end. We are truly just getting started.

Remember that social media does not exist as a marketplace for you to sell the products of your business, or shove your message down people's throats. This is never the role of social media—ever. The sales process is last, if it even enters into the social media realm at all. Gary V says, "Bring value, bring value, bring value, ask for the business." (Or *Jab, Jab, Jab, Right Hook*, which is the title of his book. Be sure to check it out.

You can find a copy anywhere books are sold or here: http://bit.ly/GaryVJJJRH.

You have to offer three "bring values" before you "ask for the business." If you were selling your wares on social media, it would be "show product, ask for the money." That is not how social media works. Social media is a platform on which you can interact with your customers and your audience. It is a place where you can tweak your message for your benefit. Politicians and the media call this kind of tweaking "spin."

For example, a brand can shape its message after finding itself mired in negative press, which has happened to a lot of brands. Maybe a company executive has done something not so hot and tarnished the brand. This can be a temporary problem, provided it is not an extreme one. Regardless of whether the brand's news is negative, social media can be used to send a different message and get people on board with it.

A great example is Buffer, which recently got hacked. Buffer shares your content at the best possible times throughout the day so that your followers and fans see your updates more often. Obviously, Buffer's management could never have foreseen their website getting hacked, but when that happened, they wrapped their arms around their community. They admitted fault and said they were extremely embarrassed. They apologized profusely, and constantly updated their community via social media as to exactly where they were in the process of resolving the situation. This was not something they "should" have done; this was something that was a "must" in order to tame the chaos that the hacking incident created.

They did not try to hide anything, or lie. They did not try to act as if it was not that big a deal. They told everyone it was a really big deal. They told their community that they knew it was a really big deal to them, and it was also a really big deal to Buffer. They assured their community that they were very committed to making sure that their platform was restored. They vowed to make everything right for their customers. That, in my opinion, is a feather in the cap of Buffer's management. They admitted fault. They did not try to hide anything. They encouraged their audience and when everything was back up and restored, they sent out e-mail to everyone, apologizing once again, and they told their customers how thankful they were to have them.

Building a brand and running a business always has been about your customers, your people. This is not going to change. Telling yourself that you "should" respond to your customers and engage with them is like saying, "I should have a marketing plan," or, "I should have a customer service department." Of course you should! You must! All of those things are essential to doing business. Engaging with your customers and responding to their feedback, negative or positive, is a must.

Social media is tied to every single department of your business. If you allow social media to be an integral part of your internal business and your employees' experience there, your brand's message will have an additional audience. Social media is tied to every single person within your organization. Social media is something that we have always done, but now we have tools and resources available to make it even easier. At this point in the chapter, if you do not understand why social media is no longer a "should" but a "must," you might want to reread the chapter, because there is nothing more to say about it. Engaging in social media is no longer a "should" for businesses—it is an absolute "must." End of story.

PRO TIP: You can do the same thing with your product or service. If you are a local business owner and people are coming into your business and checking in, you could give them something for that. That offers and creates an incredible amount of value for that customer. People just want to feel good and be heard. Make them feel good and you will give them an opportunity to say nice things about your brand, to tell people how good they feel about your brand. That is the most powerful form of marketing available.

No Listening,
No Customers

I t baffles me today when brands attempt to shove their methods
down consumers' throats as if this were 1960, when advertising with a direct message was at an all-time high. Advertising is still
very effective when done correctly. It is no longer about the push,
though. It is no longer about pushing your product and shoving your
message down customers' throats. It is now about the pull. Pulling
customers in, building a community around them, engaging with
them, listening to them, finding out what they want—that is what
advertising and marketing is today.

As my friend Bruce Turkel says, your brand is not about you. When
you pull customers in and give them good expertise or products, they
will tell their family and friends about it on a very large scale. People

love to brag. People love to get excited. Why would you make that difficult, or disrupt that process? You want to make sure that people have the platform and ability to tell anyone and everyone about your brand and about the experience they had with your brand.

We follow our favorite brands on social media because they provide value to us. They entertain us and interact with us about things we want to talk about, not just about things *they* want to talk about. Think about whether you have ever engaged with a large brand on Facebook or Twitter, or whether you have commented on the brand's blog or one of their videos. Did they respond by saying, "Thank you"? If not, they let you down.

There is nothing better than checking into a hotel on Facebook and posting a picture and having the hotel's management respond with "We're really glad you're here. We hope you enjoy your stay." That happens more often than not with me, and it always gives me a good feeling. If I am not even staying at the hotel and just happen to be there for an event, the hotel management always hits me up on Twitter and asks me how my experience was. It is very important to me. I do not care if I have been at a venue for an hour or have spent a weekend or a week there. The very fact that the brand's management pauses and asks me how I am doing solidifies my faith in what that brand is all about. Again, as my friend Bruce Turkel so brilliantly says, "A good brand makes you feel good. A great brand makes you feel good about yourself."

Location-based marketing tools such as the Foursquare app really bridged the gap between consumers and local businesses, especially consumers who did not know about a particular business. Imagine some customers shopping at a local store and when they are done shopping, they want to eat lunch within a two-mile radius of the store. But the problem is they don't know where to go, either because they don't know the area or they do know the area and they don't want to eat at the same old place. They pull up the Foursquare app. Foursquare automatically does the work for them and tells them which restaurants are within a two-mile radius of where they are. The customer finds a new discovery, eats there, loves it and returns time and time again.

If you are listed on Foursquare as a business—which you should be because it is free for brands and for consumers, and is an untapped marketplace, so why not?—you can set up check-in offers. For instance, "Come by Joe's Taco Shack. For your first visit here you can check in for a free taco." People love free stuff and they also love new stuff and new ideas. Why not give them the opportunity to find you? Because Foursquare is fairly new, chances are your competition isn't on board yet so why not stay ahead of the curve and make sure that you are?

As I said, Foursquare is a free platform. It enables you to set up a profile and offer check-in specials so that people can tell you and the world when they become your customers and get something for doing business with you. The customer who patronizes your business the most is called the mayor. The mayor gets rewarded for his loyalty in the form of specials. So with Foursquare, you are rewarding people for coming in and doing business with you for the first time and for doing business with you repeatedly.

A great example of this is the pizza restaurant La Bufala, located on South Beach, here in Miami. Every time you check in on the Foursquare app, the restaurant gives you a free bottle of house wine. That's right, an entire bottle, and they've been doing it for years. Another great example that comes to mind is Hilton's Doubletree hotel. Upon check-in at any of their hotels and on the Foursquare app, they offer you a warm, scrumptious, chocolate chip cookie.

Businesses have been able to provide a tremendous amount of value by just doing simple things such as giving somebody a free soda or a cup of coffee or a cookie in exchange for their feedback. Those things go a long way. Why? Because they make customers feel validated and special.

> **PRO TIP:** Don't be cheap about what you give customers. Knocking 10 percent off is a joke these days. Give them something you would want to receive as a new or returning customer.

Our favorite brands want us to become lifelong customers, and the way they work toward achieving that reality is by listening to us and responding to what we tell them. Guessing at what your customers want is never a good idea. You are not a psychic. If you are, e-mail me; I need you to pick my lottery numbers for me on Saturday. (But then, you already knew that.)

Asking questions is always a win-win situation, because the brand gathers useful information and the customer feels validated and respected. How do you feel when you give feedback to a brand and the brand actually listens, applies that feedback and grows or improves based on that feedback? It makes you feel good. It makes you feel as if you have been heard. It makes you feel that what you said has been validated. Never underestimate the power of validating a customer, ever.

When an angry, dissatisfied customer complains, it is a perfect opportunity for a business to correct the problem and then to go on to transform that customer into a lifelong brand ambassador. Some of the angriest customers can become lifelong brand soldiers in your volunteer army of crusaders, constantly fighting the good fight for you, preaching the gospel of how awesome your brand is to every person they know. Those are the types of people and customers you want to align yourself with. Sometimes it starts out ugly but ends up pretty, as long as you listen, respond, and offer a solution. Sometimes your angriest customer becomes your most profitable one.

As the old saying goes, there is no stronger faith than the faith of a convert. If you own a restaurant and a customer complains, invite him back for dinner on the house until he is happy. You will take a hit to your bottom line, but you will get many things in return, including a satisfied customer and positive word of mouth as the story spreads. Positive word of mouth is worth far more than your cost of a meal.

As a restaurant owner, you could focus on the revenue you are losing to a dissatisfied customer whom you have a chance of winning back, or you could focus on an even worse case: the negative word of mouth you would be enduring if you did not invite that customer back to try to win him over. If you do not invite that customer to come back at your expense, it will cost you even more money, believe me. You will lose that customer, and he will go on to tell every person he knows about his bad experience. Take the hit to your bottom line. Turn a negative situation into a positive one. The long-term financial and customer benefits are worth the short-term loss. In fact, the long-term benefits are virtually unlimited. You never know what one little act of good faith will do to a customer. You never know how it might play out, either with that customer or someone he tells about his positive experience. At the very least, by addressing a problem head-on, you will learn how to avoid it in the future.

Customers do not mind past problems as long as the problems have been resolved properly. Most times people accept the fact that not everybody or every brand is perfect. If you mess up, it is all right. But make sure that you correct what you messed up. Make sure that you make it right in the end.

Testimonials that result from the resolution of a problem are the best because they allow customers to connect with your brand emotionally. It is almost as if you want to have a problem here and there so you can turn a negative into a positive. Social media is about being human, admitting mistakes, apologizing, and then making things right. Think about how celebrities apologize (or not) on Twitter for their missteps. Businesses can take similar steps.

Five Brands That Are Doing Social Media Right

When I think about brands that are doing social media right, the first brand that comes to mind is everybody's favorite coffee shop (well, at least almost everybody's favorite coffee shop), Starbucks. I want to get deeper into the ingenious campaign of theirs that I mentioned earlier in the book. They run an ongoing campaign called "Share, Vote, Discuss, and See." This bold initiative is not designed to sell more coffee, but to provide value and listen to their community. They wanted the community to tell them how they could improve their brand. What an incredible way to tap into the resources that are already there: people who are already advocates of your brand.

Running this campaign has resulted in more than 50,000 product ideas from Starbucks customers and brand advocates. All that Starbucks had to do was stop, ask, and listen. Once the brand did that, it received 50,000 brand-new ideas that could be used to take an already successful multibillion-dollar corporation and make it even better. Again, the value of listening to your customers and asking what they want is absolutely priceless. You cannot put a number on that.

The next brand that comes to mind is Ford. Not only do I have a soft spot for Ford because I have a great relationship with the company here in South Florida, but I also know the management really care about their customers. They care so much that they involve their customers in the entire process of launching a new vehicle. In fact, my friend Scott Monty, head of Global Digital & Multimedia Communications for Ford Motor Company, was here in South Florida visiting our local Social Media Club South Florida in 2013.

He told us that Ford offers a program for app developers in which the developers have the ability to create their own app, one that could potentially find its way into the Sync System for Ford. He told us that this was an actual option that people could explore. What Ford is doing is involving its audience. Ford always runs an annual campaign with influencers. The most recent one was with the brand-new Ford Fiesta. They picked several influencers throughout the nation, gave them a brand-new Ford Fiesta for a year and, in exchange, asked them to create content and buzz about their driving experiences on a monthly basis. What a great way to market a brand-new product, enrolling people who (A) already have an audience, and (B) have a vested interest in the product.

The power of other people telling your story is far more powerful than your telling your own story will ever be. Don't get me wrong.

You still need to tell your own story. But having other people also tell it for you is valuable beyond words.

Although I am not a big fan of this next brand, Comcast, I have to give it credit. I do not like it for a couple of reasons. One is that Comcast has monopolized most geographic areas where they operate and most of us don't have any choice but to give them our business. It is 2014. We all need high-speed Internet access and we love HD television with that little DVR thingy that lets us skip through commercials. When my friend Frank Eliason worked for Comcast, he developed a customer-care social media program called "Comcast Cares." It enabled Comcast to respond to its customers via Twitter and other social media. This was extremely valuable. The last thing you want to do when you have a billing issue or a technical problem with your cable or Internet service is pick up the phone and spend half of the day dialing an 800 number and being put on hold with some ridiculous elevator music that makes you want to kick a puppy.

It's nice to be able to successfully reach out to a large brand such as Comcast when there is a problem, and this is something I have done consistently. I mentioned this in an earlier chapter. I was not naming the brand before, so I just let the cat out of the bag. Why? Because this time I'm giving the company praise. The company did a great job with customer service. As far as the company's overall rates and general service goes, that is a whole different chapter. But I am talking, in particular, about brands that are doing social media right. Comcast gets it when it comes to listening and responding.

Remember the Super Bowl in 2013 when the lights went out? With Oreo, we have another brand that really got it right when that happened. This brand's real-time campaign of "It's OK to Dunk in the Dark" was very well played. What Oreo did in response to that blackout is called real-time marketing. I don't care how many executives were in the room or how many people from the marketing team were in the room during the Super Bowl. I don't care how much planning went into it. It happened and in my opinion it was genius! You will probably never, ever forget that campaign, especially if you are an Oreo fan.

The bottom line is the Oreo team absolutely nailed it. Who would ever have thought the lights were going to go out in the Super Bowl? Who at Oreo would ever have thought they would have to conceptualize a real-time campaign that would enable them to push a message out that was so relevant to the lights-out crisis at that game?

Everyone watching the game was wondering what was going on, and meanwhile, Oreo's team was working diligently behind the scenes to create a campaign they knew would be relevant to what was happening in the moment. Well done, Oreo.

The online shoe retailer Zappos.com is another brand that is really doing it right. I had an opportunity to meet Zappos CEO Tony Hsieh, whose company is pretty famous for its customer service and overall customer experience. This is a company that said, "We're going to take shoes and we're going to sell them online." The last thing you want to buy online is shoes—that is, until you come into contact with a brand like Zappos. Zappos has an incredible ability to reach a customer and make him happy. In Hsieh's book, *Delivering Happiness*, he talks about creating a company culture that in turn creates a customer culture. When you have those two things together and everything is in sync, you will have a successful business. Zappos is a very successful business, for these reasons and many others.

When *Delivering Happiness* was released, instead of doing a normal book tour, Hsieh decided to paint a bus, name it "Delivering Happiness" and tour the country in it with a publicity team that he had put together. But every time they went to a new city for one of Tony's book signings, they would do something good. They were taking that bus city to city and literally delivering happiness. By default, people were buying Tony's book and getting a chance to meet him. I had the unique opportunity to attend the party at their Miami Beach stop. It was an awesome, cabana-like, poolside party on a Saturday afternoon. Tony is one of the coolest guys I have ever met. He asked me what makes me happy. The next thing I knew, members of his team were walking around handing out sticky notes and markers for people to finish the phrase: "This makes me happy …"

People wrote specifically what made them happy on their sticky notes. I wrote, "Spearmint gum." Tony said, "Really? When was the last time you had a piece?" None of this is relevant except that his stopping and taking an interest in what I said was very interesting—and he responded accordingly. You could tell he cared about the conversation he was having with me. Having that same mindset with your brand is so important.

Zappos gets it when it comes to customer service. It's no mystery. Tony has found success with this company and it is constantly growing. People cannot get enough of it. The bottom line is, if you buy a pair of shoes and they don't fit, you ship them back free of charge and Zappos sends you a new pair until the shoe fits. I heard a story about a drunk who called Zappos, thinking it was a pizza delivery place. The Zappos customer service rep didn't hang up on that caller; he or she actually put him on hold, called a local pizza place, and ordered a pizza for him. The drunk guy was not even a customer of Zappos. Talk about delivering happiness. Talk about going above and beyond when you clearly do not have to, even for somebody who is not giving you business.

I heard another story about Zappos and the company's welcoming spirit. If you are ever in Las Vegas and you want to check out the Zappos compound, they will send a car to the airport to pick you up. They will bring you to the corporate office, give you a full tour of the entire operation, and Tony Hsieh will set aside an hour to sit down and talk to you, answering any questions you have about the Zappos brand. Wowza! Well done, Zappos!

You talk about the "speed of the leader," or "speed of the pack," and Tony exemplifies that. He is consistently able to deliver a message to the world and also help people better understand what his brand is all about. No matter how big Zappos gets, Tony never seems to be too cool for anyone. The brand name never seems to be too big for its britches. Zappos, I commend you for what you are doing. You are not slowing down by any means at all, and it is no mystery why you have been so successful. Anyone who has not bought a pair of shoes or a clothing item from Zappos.com is really missing out.

These are just five examples of brands that are actually doing it right. You are probably thinking, "Yeah, they've got billions of dollars; they'd better be doing it right." That is not always the case. It does not matter if you have thousands of dollars or millions of dollars. If you are not treating your customers right, you are throwing money away. Listening, responding, engaging, and doing things right is the lifeblood of a business. It is the key to making sure you have a long-term, sustainable brand. Why? Remember, word-of-mouth is completely scalable. It has always been around, but it is even more scalable these days with social media.

If you are not doing things right, people are going to be talking about you and letting other people know that you are not doing things right. They always say "Any press is good press," but I'm not sure how true that is these days when people can rake you over the coals if you provide them with a negative experience. The bottom line is, do the right thing and you will get the right results.

> **PRO TIP:** Find a way to allow your brand to stand out by your creative use of Social Media, even if you're not a large brand like ones mentioned above.

Bring Value, Bring Customers

I know I have talked about Gary Vaynerchuk several times throughout this book, but his information, his insight, and his ability to constantly think ahead of the game boggles my mind. He is so dead-on every single time. One of his favorite sayings is, "Bring value, bring value, bring value, ask for the business." The title of his brand new book, *Jab, Jab, Jab, Right Hook*, essentially says the same thing. This is perfectly relevant to what you should be doing in your social media strategies. You should be building a community, engaging in that community, listening to that community, wrapping your arms around that community, pulling that community in, providing value and, by default, earning the opportunity to "ask for the business." If you do all of that, the sales process will take care of itself, because you have earned it. If people need what you have, they are going to buy it anyway. They are going to be even more inclined to do so if you are providing value to them, and value starts with listening and actually caring.

People want to know the who, what, why, and where of your business before making a buying decision, but they also want to be sure that they know, like and trust you. They want that information immediately, like yesterday. When consumers feel that the information you are providing on social media is valuable, they apply that value judgment to your overall brand as well. They are evaluating your customer service and they are evaluating the value that you offer, meaning the content you provide for them on social media.

You want customers to say, "You know what? That brand did this for me before I ever gave them a dollar." That is value. Maybe it is answering a question, maybe it is doing something off the cuff or offering a real-time response, but it comes back to doing something extra. People see that. People feel that, and it resonates with them. You could have a customer who is on the fence about his decision to do business with you. Instead of asking him to send his payment, or asking him how he would like to take care of payment, maybe you could provide him some additional information. That could push him completely over the fence and into your side of the yard. Why? Because he will have seen that you provided him with something before you ever got something for yourself, and that is the name of the game.

Over the past three years, while I built my brand from literally nothing other than using social media, all I had to provide was content and some of what I knew about social media. I have built my brand on providing value to people and expecting nothing in return. There is an old Zig Ziglar quote:

"You will get all you want in life, if you help enough other people get what they want."

I believe that wholeheartedly. I sure as heck did not have a bunch of money to start this company, and I could not pay people to help me, but I could compensate them with knowledge. I could help them understand what they "didn't know they didn't know" about social media.

I have helped people better understand what Facebook, Twitter, YouTube, and blogs are. I have shared videos and experiences of events that have pertained to my brand. I have shared interviews with other influencers like Gary Vaynerchuk, Guy Kawasaki, Jay Baer, and Scott Monty—guys who are thought leaders in the digital and social space who know more about social media than I could ever start to imagine. I provide this information to my audience, and they look to me as a valuable, go-to source when it comes to social media.

Every time I see old friends, especially if I have not seen them in a long time, I seem to consistently hear: "Wow, you are everywhere." That makes me feel good because I know if I am out there making noise, people will be knocking on my door. People get curious about what you are doing because they see that you are everywhere, and providing value. I knew that if I got out there and kept swinging and staying in people's faces and wearing a bow tie, people would not forget me. It was Steve Martin who once said, "Be so good they can't ignore you." I think that is an amazing philosophy for a brand. That is what I've strived to do since day one. Whether it is through a bow tie, or high energy, helping people better understand what they "don't know they don't know" about social media or all of the above, I want to be so good they can't forget me, let alone ignore me.

When you go overboard with value and help, when you go overboard with pulling and not pushing, you will come out winning every single time. That is what providing value is all about. Gary V once said, "If you're willing to leave a little bit of money on the table, you will close every deal."

I built a brand with nothing other than providing value and striving to be the go-to source for people when it came to social media. It excites me to know that I was the obvious choice for people who wanted to learn more about social media and how they could create buzz for their brand. You can do the same thing. Provide value. Start a blog. Comment on threads that pertain to your interests. Share other people's information. Retweet other people's information. The world of social media and sharing content is not the world of narcissism. If you want to succeed and you want people to share your content and grow your community, make sure that you are growing other people's community and sharing their content too. Again, I'll quote Gary V as I close this chapter: "Jab, jab, jab, right hook"—that is, "Bring value, bring value, bring value, ask for the business."

Daily Deals:
The Right Way and
the Wrong Way

First of all, what is a daily deal campaign? You may have heard a daily deal referred to as a Groupon, which is like calling a facial tissue a Kleenex, or a photocopy machine a Xerox. To most people, a daily deal is a Groupon, whether it is offered by Living Social or another local daily deal in a newspaper or some other local publication. Daily deals have revolutionized the way consumers interact with local businesses. They also have revolutionized the way local businesses can bring new customers through their door every single day. The problem? Business owners get it all wrong. They think a Groupon, a daily deal, or a Living Social deal is simply run to give them a spike in sales, but during that spike they will be forfeiting 40 to 60 percent of their profit margin. They see this as losing. But it is absolutely not losing; in fact, it's far from it.

Guess what? If you are selling a product for a dollar and you have to pay 50 cents to get a customer through the door to buy it the first time, but the customer keeps coming back and buying it for full price, that is called winning. I cannot stress enough how vital daily deals are to businesses. Number one, they do not cost anything right off the bat. You do not have to pay for a marketing and advertising campaign. You are paying for every brand-new customer who comes through the door. You are paying roughly half of their tab.

So sure, you have to give up 40 to 60 percent of your profit margin when you agree to offer a daily deal, but you would never, otherwise, have had that customer. And there is a chance you will turn that customer into a repeat customer or even a regular, lifelong customer. That is a gamble worth taking. But you need to make sure that you can deliver on what you are offering in your daily deal. Too many businesses enter into a daily deal platform and overwhelm themselves. For instance, if you own a salon that has only two nail technicians and you decide to run a daily deal campaign on manicures to a million people, chances are you are going to get overwhelmed. You are not going to be able to balance that business, and that is not a good thing.

Make sure that the campaign you are offering matches up with your manpower and/or inventory. The last thing you want to do is sell 1,000 units when you have only 200 units in your garage. That scenario would create a significant problem for you and your brand. Running a daily deal and giving up 40 to 60 percent of your profit margin to get new customers through the door is not creating a problem for your brand. It is one of the best things that can ever happen to your brand. Why? You are teaming up with one of the largest platforms out there, whether it is Groupon, Living Social, Gilt City, or one of the other daily deal providers.

The bottom line is, you are collaborating with a large brand that has the ability to reach the people you want to talk to. Daily deals sell people your product or service without your having to do anything other than take part in the deal. It is your job, once the deal is sold, to greet the customers when they come in, to welcome them as daily deal customers and tell them that you are really glad that they took advantage of that awesome offer. It is your job to keep the customers there, and convince them to come back.

Give them something else. Give them something to drink if they come into your location. I worked with a client here in South Florida who operates an outdoor center within a local park. They rent kayaks and bikes and also have a restaurant right outside the park. They ran a daily deal that let people go on a 90-minute kayak ride and then have lunch. They got an incredible response, selling more than 1,500 deals during the campaign. The only challenge was the amount of manpower they had at the restaurant and the amount of kayaks they had. It was not a huge issue, but a couple of people had to wait a little bit longer for their lunch after their kayak ride and they got a little upset. Again, a couple of people out of 1,500. I will take that all day long.

They had great success with that daily deal. Why? They offered something of value to people here in South Florida. People like to get outdoors. People like to eat. Those are two things that really allowed them to have a tremendous amount of success, but I told them, "If we're really going to capitalize on running a deal with Living Social, we need to make sure that we're capturing information from the people who are coming through here. We want to make sure that we're staying in touch with these people."

We put signs all over the facility where people came to check in, and especially near the check-in desk itself. We wanted to make sure that they checked in on Foursquare. If they checked in on Foursquare, they would get a free water bottle coozy. If they checked in on Facebook, we would give them a free granola bar. These are just simple little things that allowed us to give them something in exchange for their doing something for us. It was also a way for us to stay in touch with them. We also had them write down their name and e-mail address when they came to claim their daily deal. That allowed us to continue to stay in touch with them and market to them, specifically, as daily deal customers.

> **PRO TIP:** A great way of capturing new and existing customers' e-mails is to create a Facebook tab. Most bulk e-mail providers, such as Constant Contact and MailChimp, offer a turnkey tab solution in which you can create a tab by simply logging in to your e-mail marketing account with your provider and following a few simple steps. Try Googling "Add MailChimp (or Constant Contact) tab to Facebook." It's a very simple process.

We stayed in touch with the customers who came to us through the daily deal. Since we gave them a deal the first time around—the daily deal itself—we didn't have to give them a subsequent deal that was 40 to 60 percent off. But we could give them a follow-up e-mail offering them the opportunity to return and experience our brand again, and all we had to do was give them $5 or $10 off. A gesture like that still makes people feel special. It still makes people feel they are getting a deal.

Think about how you feel when you get a deal on something. Think about going to a flea market. If something is marked at $50 and you walk away with it for $35, you are pretty excited. Maybe it is the thrill of negotiating. Maybe it is just being able to save a little money. The bottom line is we all get excited when we get a deal. The best way to invite a customer back is to give him something for free in addition to a special offer in which he will spend money with you.

That is what daily deals do. Think of it this way. When daily deal customers walk through your door, you are not losing 40 to 60 percent of your profit margin. You are creating an opportunity to gain lifelong customers. It is your job to keep them there. Make sure you capture their e-mail addresses. Make sure you get them to like your page on Facebook. Make sure you get them to follow you on Twitter. Make sure you get them to subscribe to your other platforms when they are there in your presence.

People like and need to be told what to do. You can't assume that they already know how to connect with you. Having their e-mail addresses and having them connected to all of your social platforms allows you to stay in touch with them. It allows you to keep the conversation going and it is your job to make that conversation happen—at least to get it started. You must stay in touch with them. I recommend that you market to them as a specific daily deal customer. People like to feel unique. Make sure that you create that experience for them.

If they bought one deal with Living Social or Groupon, market to them as a "Valued Groupon Customer" or a "Valued Living Social Customer." This enables and empowers them. It makes them feel special and part of the club. Make them feel they are not just part of the general population of your customers. Let them know that they are in a niche group. Get them excited about being a customer of yours. When people feel excited about a brand that they know, like, and trust, they are even more inclined to tell their friends about it and share that excitement.

Many people confuse daily deals with a get-rich-quick campaign, and they are far from that. Daily deals are more like meet-new-people campaigns. Do you lose all of your money when you sell a product or service through a daily deal platform such as Groupon or Living Social? Absolutely not. Are you making 100 percent profit on it? Absolutely not. What is the value of meeting a new customer who comes through your door and gives you the ability to stay in touch with him? The value is that you can continue to market to him and possibly turn him into a brand ambassador. He could become somebody who joins your volunteer army and constantly talks about what your brand does and how awesome it is. Can you really put a price tag on that? That is powerful stuff. That is the power of a daily deal.

Sometimes, daily deals do not go as anticipated. Social media can come into play in this situation too. Social media can help you explain the problems that occurred in your daily deal experiment. Maybe you underestimated quantities on the deal that you ran. Maybe you did not have as many cupcakes as you thought you had. Maybe you could not produce enough cupcakes to fulfill all of the orders on time. Before you decide to do a daily deal, make sure that the deal is structured in a way that allows you a little bit of a buffer. Say something like "If we get X amount of response, the product will be delivered by X date."

If you run a deal on Wednesday offering a dozen cupcakes free with the purchase of a dozen cupcakes and you promise to fulfill all orders by Saturday, you might have a problem. Make sure you have enough time to fill the orders. Make sure that all of the customers' expectations are laid out and clearly understood when they buy the deal. That is going to save you a lot of headaches and it is going to prevent people from coming back and saying, "I want the deal that I purchased."

If the customers understand everything going into the daily deal, it is kind of like ordering something on television way back when. The television offer would be made with a condition, something like "Please allow four to six weeks for delivery." What was the best thing to do? Order it, hang up the phone and forget about it. When it showed up at your doorstep, at least you expected it to take that long to arrive. Make sure your daily deals are extremely clear when you run them. There is no better way to upset customers than to let them think they are buying one thing, but they end up getting something else, or nothing at all. In the event that you do have challenges, allow people to Tweet and post on Facebook, or message you—good, bad, or indifferent. It goes back to customer service.

> **PRO TIP:** If customers are irate and messaging complaints publicly, ask them to private-message you their phone number, e-mail address, and other contact information. This way, you can continue the conversation in a more discreet, professional manner without adversely affecting your brand.

You've got to take the good with the bad. Let customers respond to you and send you feedback, even if it is negative. Do something for them. Give them something, and yes, give them something for free. If they're already there, you're probably thinking, "They've bought a Groupon. As it is, it's already costing me 40 to 60 percent right off the top, and I've got to give them a free hot dog?" Absolutely. Do you want them to leave happy? Yes, you do. Do you want them to talk to other people about you, and talk about how it was a challenging process, but you went above and beyond to make the situation right? Yes, you do. Daily deals, social media, and customer service—those three working together all at the same time are great.

Now, let's talk about the positive side of social media as it relates to daily deals. Let's say somebody gets a really stellar deal. They experience your brand, product, or service. They have a great time, and they want to tell people about it. That happened a lot during the outdoor center campaign we ran with Living Social. People would post pics of themselves out on a kayak, and then they would post pics of themselves eating lunch at the restaurant right outside the park. They were really excited about the experience. When your customers do things like that, you want to first thank them for sharing their experience, and then you want to share their content with your network. When people see that other people are engaging with your brand, and it is a brand they are not familiar with, it piques their interest. When people's interest is piqued, they think about becoming one of your customers, especially when other customers are excited about your brand and telling the world about it.

This is how the viral effect continues to take place within social media. I go and experience a brand. I like it and I share it with my network. The brand shares my content with its network. People within the network see that there are happy customers, and people within my network see that I am happy. All of it leads to more people getting exposed to the brand. That is the power of social media and daily deals.

How does a business choose the right daily platform? You do not have to worry about which platform is the best fit for your brand. When you pitch one of these daily deal platforms, whether it is with Gilt City, Living Social, or Groupon, you are going to propose the deal you want to run with them. They may tweak it or they may just shoot you down altogether. They get hundreds upon hundreds of requests every single day. There is a good, solid lead time for deals, too. You need a solid month, or month and a half, I would say, to be able to structure the deal, negotiate the deal, and get the deal up and running. It takes about a solid month-plus, start-to-finish, so make sure that you plan for that. They will tell you right away whether or not they are going to take your offer, so it is not a matter of asking, "Which one should I go with?" Have the deal ready before you approach them. Make sure you can deliver on the deal and then get ready for scads of new customers to walk through your door.

If you have offers available on more than one daily deal platform, most times the deals will need to be different. Most daily deal providers will not let you run the same deal simultaneously with their competitors. In that case, you should choose the deal that is most advantageous to you. Which discount percentage is lower, and what are you getting more of? How many people are they marketing to? What is the reach within the campaign? These are all factors that will help you decide which daily deal platform is best for you. In my opinion, Groupon and Living Social are the industry leaders, but it really comes down to personal preference and who offers you the best deal.

Remember—it does not matter if the cut into your profit is 40 or 60 percent, as long as you get new customers through the door. Getting brand-new customers through your door, customers you did not know yesterday, is extremely valuable. Get excited about them. Let them get excited about you. They will tell people about you. When they tell people about you, other people will become interested in you, so you have gained not one customer but maybe multiple customers. The opportunities are endless when it comes to daily deals as long as you are doing them correctly and understanding the value of giving up a percentage of your profit to run the deal. When you get those new customers through the door, wrap your arms around them, pull them in and tell them how excited you are to meet them and have them as new customers. They will appreciate that, they will thank you for that, and they will tell their friends and family about that.

Social Media Ties It All Together

For years, people have made a conscious decision to do business with people and brands that they "know, like and trust." Why? The reason is quite simple. It makes them feel comfortable about the buying decisions they are making. I am going to get into each category and break it down, but gaining a customer's trust should be at the forefront of every single business and brand. Let's break down the "know, like, and trust" concepts individually.

KNOW

Your customers know you because they have connected with you online. They have found you on their own, or they have been marketed to, or someone recommended you to them. This is the first step in earning a customer: being introduced in one way or another. If your content is sexy enough, or valuable enough, they will feel they have been friends with you for years. They will talk about you like family. This is clearly what each and every brand should strive for.

Ask yourself these vital questions:
1. How can I get people to join my volunteer army?
2. How do I acquire brand advocates?
3. How do I give them what they want?

LIKE

Facebook has shed an entirely new light on this word *like*. It fascinates me that they use a word that has been part of the English language for as long as we can remember, yet, today, it has an almost automatic association with the Facebook brand. Think about what makes you "like" something. It is an emotional decision that you make because that something makes you feel good. You connect with that brand or message. When you like something, what do you normally do? You talk about it. This is the powerful part of people liking you: they will talk about you! How do you get them to like you? You get them to like you by providing exactly what they want to read and hear. You get them to like you by helping them when you do not have to help. You get them to like you by showing them that they now know you and you know them. You get them to like you by providing value, by providing value, by providing value. Did I mention you get them to like you by providing value?

TRUST

This is the most important component of the three. If people do not trust your voice and brand, they will never commit. Think about personal relationships. Would you ever tell one of your deep dark secrets to someone you do not trust? Most likely not. The same applies in business. We all know every relationship is built on trust. It takes years to build trust and it can take only seconds to break it. You have got to have an authentic, value-based relationship with your customers. They have to know that they can trust you. They have to know that if they have a problem, you are going to resolve it. They have to know that if they have a good or bad experience, you are going to have their back. They have to know that if they need you, you are there for them. Trust is earned, not given. It is the same in life as it is in business.

Use this game plan and people will know, like, and trust your brand. When they do that, they will talk to other people about it, and endorse it. They will share the gospel of your brand, and most importantly, they will buy and consume your product.

When I think about SocialBuzzTV.com, my own brand, I have "know, like and trust" in the forefront of my mind all the time. If I find somebody who piques my interest, I want to know that person. When people want to learn about social media and how they can create a buzz for their brand, they want to get to know me. I embrace the power of getting to know people. I am always open to connecting, meeting new people, and finding out exactly what we can do to help each other in building each other's brands and lives.

As Gary V would argue, "authenticity trumps likability." Authenticity is a major component of building trust in any relationship. People ultimately do business with people they trust to get the job done. Sure, being likable is important. If people don't like you, they are not going to do business with you. They are not going to consume your brand or product unless it is a unique niche product that they cannot get anywhere else. In that case, they will deal with you, even though they don't really like you. That is a very rare situation. I do not do business with people that I don't jive with. There has to be a mutual flow. Always have it in the forefront of your mind to be likable. I am always excited about knowing that people like what I am doing. I always get excited to like what somebody else is doing. Liking is extremely powerful and I apply it to my brand personally and professionally as much as I possibly can. However; people ultimately want to do business with people they like AND trust. If they like you yet don't fully trust you, they won't do business with you.

Trust. Again, without trust, there is no relationship. I want my clients to know that when they pay me to do something, I am going to deliver on it. They trust that I am going to deliver on it. Most of the time, the majority of my agency's clients are too busy to understand what we are truly doing until they sit down and go over reports. This helps them understand exactly what we have been doing to increase their presence, provide value, and engage with the online community on their behalf. They do not have time to sit and monitor every single aspect of their social media strategy every day, but they trust that our work speaks for itself and we deliver. It is a good thing we do, or we would be out of business.

"Know, like, and trust" is at the forefront of not only my personal brand but also of my professional brand. It is absolutely vital to the lifeblood of every single brand out there. "Know, like, and trust" has always been around and it always will be around. Embrace these three tactics and keep them at the forefront of your mind, and you will always be ten steps ahead of the game.

Social Media and the Opportunity to Pay It Forward

I f you want people to share and engage in your content, share and engage in theirs. That is the rule of reciprocity. Give, and you get. Love, and you are loved. Share, and you will be shared.

With social media, that is really what it is all about. If you want people to share your content, share theirs. If you want to get retweeted, make sure you are retweeting people's content. That is very important.

Too many people live in the land of narcissism when it comes to social media. They think their voice is the only voice. They think it is a one-way street. They think, "I am going to tell you what I have got to talk about, and I don't care what you want to talk about."

It just does not work that way. It's a two-way street. People share information. You comment, engage, like, and share that information. You talk about information. People share, like, and engage with your information. That is just the way it works.

I have always been interested in sharing content that interests me. It is just natural for me to share it. If you stick to that simple philosophy, you will always operate in a sincere and genuine space, and people will notice that. At times, there is nothing wrong with sharing content from people you simply want to connect with. In that case, the sharing is a means to an end. However, this cannot be the normal way you operate. This is reserved for special circumstances.

> PRO TIP: Social media is like adrenaline for your bottom line. It allows you to have that extra edge, that ability to build a community and have it remain top of mind among your community. It gives you the opportunity to share information with your community. It gives you the opportunity to engage with new members of your community, and it allows you to find new friends, followers, and people who want to be part of your community. This all happens through the sharing process.

Another huge aspect of leveraging social media with your brand is tying a mission to it. I happened to make the mission of Social-BuzzTV.com the launch of a local Christian church ministry in the Wynwood art district of Miami. Never in a million years did I think I would be involved in the start-up of a church in the Miami area, but as my journey first started with SocialBuzzTV.com, I quickly found out that was where my passion lay.

I wanted to take an opportunity, a dream, and turn it into a reality. Most importantly, I wanted to leverage my brand and my SocialBuzzTV.com exposure to spread the word. I wanted to use the exposure and the reach that I had with SocialBuzzTV.com to help this church launch.

Depending on your religious preference, maybe starting a church is not something you would have in mind. That is okay. To each his own.

> **PRO TIP:** When you have a mission for your brand, your brand is more than just about you and your bottom line. Tying a mission to your brand allows you to let people know that you care about something deeper, not just about your business.

How do you find a mission for your brand? It is fairly simple. Find something that you are extremely passionate about. Maybe you like to feed people in a soup kitchen. Maybe you like to help the homeless. Maybe you like to visit sick children or tutor underprivileged children. Maybe you just like to go to a nursing home and visit people.

You could support a large organization, such as Susan G. Komen for the Cure, or the American Cancer Society. Whatever your passion may be, you can tie your business to it.

Alexandra Figueredo (@OnAMissionAlex) does an incredible job at this and has built an entire company around mission-based branding. Her agency, the Mission Based Branding Institute (MissionBasedBranding.com), creates opportunities and branding strategies for clients, allowing them to align themselves with a mission and something they are passionate about. The way it usually works is a portion of a brand's revenue goes to a charity or organization on a monthly or annual basis. When people see this message, it resonates with them.

Think about TOMS, the large shoe brand. This company is exceptional at mission-based branding and responsible for probably one of the largest mission-based campaigns to date. How it works is this: if you buy a pair of TOMS shoes, the company will gift a pair of shoes to somebody who has no shoes. People get that. They identify with it. Why? We all wear shoes, number one. Number two, we all know that there are people in this world who cannot afford shoes.

You can do the same thing with your brand. You can align your brand with a mission. Think about what you are passionate about, contact an organization that does that kind of work, and let that organization know you would like to partner with it. Offer a portion of your proceeds to them. When you operate a mission-based brand, people see that you are about more than just yourself and your business profits. In addition, you can leverage your connection with your mission to gain exposure for both you and the mission. You scratch the mission's back; it scratches yours. The mission staff will love the fact that you are donating a portion of your revenue to their organization and, in turn, they are going to love to talk about you.

Having a mission-based brand, in my opinion, is absolutely vital in 2014 and beyond. A lot of the large brands and businesses operating today contribute to charity and give back to the community, but their messages are not emphasized as much as I think they could be. I am starting to talk about this more and more in the social media presentations I give.

In fact, Alexandra and I gave a talk titled "How to Be Social and Socially Responsible as a Brand" at Social Media Day Miami in 2013. It was extremely well received. We helped people understand exactly what they needed to do for their brand to be social, and we explained exactly what they needed to know about making their brand socially responsible.

We offered case studies, such as TOMS and Warby Parker, an eyeglasses company that gives eyeglasses to someone who cannot afford them each time a Warby Parker customer buys a pair. People identify with these kinds of initiatives. They approve of them. How could they not? People wear glasses. They wear shoes. They recognize these brands. Most importantly, it starts to make them think about having a mission for their brand.

It is all about paying it forward. It is all about going into every situation, every scenario, and finding out what you can do to help. Once you do that, you will receive everything you need to achieve your goals and, often, more. Sometimes, you are passionate about something but there is no organization out there to pair up with your brand. If that is the case, create your own organization and make that your mission.

That is what I decided to do. Never in a million years did I think SocialBuzzTV.com was going to be a mission-based brand until the opportunity presented itself. I felt extremely strong about the opportunity that was presented to me, so I knew that it was something I had to pursue. I knew that it was something I had the wherewithal to create.

At the time of writing this book, we are only a year and a half into this mission, but in one year we have seen growth, and we have seen SocialBuzzTV.com evolve into a true mission-based brand. If you do not have a charity organization that resonates with you, create your own. Just make sure that your mission gives back and impacts the lives of the individuals you are supporting.

CONCLUSION

I've said this all before, so I'll repeat it here:

Social media is no longer a "should," it is a "must." I have been explicit about this. In the past everyone said, "I should be doing social media," or, "I should be doing this with my brand." As Tony Robbins so brilliantly put it, people end up "shoulding" all over themselves.

Social media is a must. Social media is a must. Social media is a must. That's right. I just said it three times. I think we are clear. Any business or brand not engaging in social media today will soon be left behind. In 1999, Bill Gates said, "If you don't have a website on the Internet in the year 2000 you are not in business." I believe that was true. We are now into 2014 and if your brand is not social today, you are not in business. You can quote me on that one.

Social media can help you do three things.

- Number one, it can help you build a community.
- Number two, it allows you to engage with that community.
- Number three, it can make you that go-to source in your community or industry.

When these three things happen, you remain top of mind within your community and among your people. That is extremely powerful. You cannot put a price tag on that.

- **Being social is nothing new.** Imagine the days of cavemen, when people sat around a fire and communicated about the dangers or delights of their surroundings. Think about the early stages of the telephone, or the fax machine, the beeper or the cell phone. Those were just new types of technology that allowed us to do the same old thing: be social.

- **We are social every day.** We are social when we walk out of our houses and say hello to our neighbors. We are social when we walk into a local coffee shop and greet a barista. We say hello to the mailman when he walks by. When we engage in business with our employees, our clients, our prospects, the people we network with, that is all social media. We just have all of these amazing tools now that were not here eight years ago. They are now at our fingertips and they enable us to connect with people instantaneously.

- **We are in the midst of an amazing shift in the way we communicate.** Now is the time to capitalize on that by leveraging our opportunity to use these tools. The majority of major social media networks out there are free to use. The only real challenge is actually sitting down and using them. We used to look for news and information. We used to let our fingers do the walking as the *Yellow Pages* directory told us to do. These days, news and information comes directly to us. News and information breaks on Twitter before it breaks on major news outlets. That should tell you something. Just as Gary Vaynerchuk so ingeniously said (and I repeat this almost on a daily basis): **"Social media is overthrowing governments in the Middle East. Do you really have the audacity to think it's not affecting your business?"** Our desire to be social and communicate has never lost its appeal. In fact, it has only increased. The fact that every human being is never more than three feet away from his or her cell phone should tell us that. We are highly addicted to the digital space. Every time someone comments, likes or shares our status, it gives us a rush of happiness, validates us, and makes us feel excited.

- **It goes back and forth constantly.** We share; people share. We like; people like. We comment; people comment. We share this back and forth exchange of information almost instantaneously. That is extremely powerful. Knowing that people are operating at light speed, adapting to new forms of communication and technology all the time, should make any business owner or prospective owner ecstatic. The intense rate at which word of mouth travels on social media alone is enough to make a business owner giddy. Maybe you have not even started a brand. Maybe you have been thinking about it. Maybe you have been sitting in your cubicle at your office, miserable, wanting to quit your job. **Well, I am here to tell you that social media creates phenomenal opportunities.** There has never been a more exciting or easy time to start a business than right now. Social media is readily available for you to connect, build a community, engage with that community, and become that go-to source for what you do. You can walk in and tell your boss you quit.

Disclosure: I am not telling you to quit your job. I am just telling you that life is too short to do stuff that does not make you happy.

Today, our messages spread great distances instantly, and listening to what is being said on social media is often more important than spreading your message on it. **Social media is not a sales device.** Social media is not there for you to shove your message down consumers' throats. Remember—advertising and marketing is push, push, push. "Here's my message, here's my message, here's my message

..." **Social media is pull, pull, pull.** "I want to pull you in and get you into my ecosystem."

How do you pull people in? You build a community around them. You engage and listen to them, and you give them what they want. You let them know that their opinion counts. You are effectively pulling them in. If you pull them in, there is no need to push your message. They will already know what it is because they will already be engaged with you.

Social media is not going away. The Genie is not going back in the bottle. Why not get involved in it at the highest level today and make it work for you? Every means of communication technology that has helped improve our lives was at one time on the fringe and largely not adopted. All of it went from being a "should" to a "must." Again, this is where we are with social media today, right on that cusp.

Too many people still underestimate the power of social media. It is in its infancy. But make no mistake—it is alive and well. Social media may be an infant but it is a healthy, growing infant, 100 percent alive. That excites me to no end. We are truly just getting started.

How can you use this book?

MOTIVATE

EDUCATE

THANK

INSPIRE

PROMOTE

CONNECT

Why have a custom version of *Social Media SUCKS!*

- Build personal bonds with customers, prospects, employees, donors, and key constituencies
- Develop a long-lasting reminder of your event, milestone, or celebration
- Provide a keepsake that inspires change in behavior and change in lives
- Deliver the ultimate "thank you" gift that remains on coffee tables and bookshelves
- Generate the "wow" factor

Books are thoughtful gifts that provide a genuine sentiment that other promotional items cannot express. They promote employee discussions and interaction, reinforce an event's meaning or location, and they make a lasting impression. Use your book to say "Thank You" and show people that you care.

www.ingramcontent.com/pod-product-compliance
Lightning Source LLC
Jackson TN
JSHW011950131224
75386JS00042B/1648